FOOD LOVERS

A TASTE OF ASIA

FOOD LOVERS

A TASTE
OF ASIA

RECIPES SELECTED BY MARIE CLAYTON

Trans
Atlantic
Press

All recipes serve four people, unless otherwise indicated.

For best results when cooking the recipes in this book, buy fresh ingredients and follow the instructions carefully. Make sure that everything is properly cooked through before serving, particularly any meat and shellfish, and note that as a general rule vulnerable groups such as the very young, elderly people and pregnant women should avoid dishes that contain raw eggs. Take care when cooking with chilies, If slicing or chopping chilies, it is a wise precaution to wear disposable plastic gloves. Take care not to touch your eyes if you have been handling chilies.

For all recipes, quantities are given in standard U.S. cups and imperial measures, followed by the metric equivalent. Follow one set or the other, but not a mixture of both because conversions may not be exact. Standard spoon and cup measurements are level and are based on the following:

1 tsp = 5 ml, 1 tbsp = 15 ml, 1 cup = 250 ml / 8 fl oz.

Note that Australian standard tablespoons are 20 ml, so Australian readers should use 3 tsp in place of 1 tbsp when measuring small quantities.

The electric oven temperatures in this book are given for conventional ovens with top and bottom heat. When using a fan oven, the temperature should be decreased by about 20–40°F / 10–20°C – check the oven manufacturer's instruction book for further guidance.

CONTENTS

MAIN COURSES:
MEAT AND POULTY DISHES 88–173

SOUPS

SWEETCORN AND CRAB MEAT SOUP

Ingredients

1 egg white

1 tsp sesame oil

4 cups / 1 liter chicken broth (stock)

2 cups / 400 g drained canned or thawed frozen corn

1 tbsp rice wine or dry sherry

1 tbsp light soy sauce

2 inch / 5 cm piece fresh ginger root, peeled and grated

1 tsp sugar

Salt and freshly ground pepper, to taste

2 tsp cornstarch (cornflour), mixed to a smooth paste in 1 tbsp water

1½ cups / 250 g flaked crabmeat, picked over to remove shells

To garnish:

2 scallions (spring onions), thinly sliced

1 tbsp chopped cilantro (fresh coriander) leaves

Method
Prep and cook time: 30 min

1 In a small bowl, whisk together the egg white and sesame oil; set aside.

2 Bring the broth (stock) to a boil in a large saucepan. Add the corn and simmer for around 4 minutes.

3 Add the rice wine or sherry, soy sauce, ginger, sugar, and a little salt and pepper; heat through.

4 Stir in the cornstarch (cornflour) mixture and bring to a boil, then add the crab.

5 Slowly add the egg white mixture, stirring constantly; heat through and season with salt and pepper. Serve garnished with scallions (spring onion) and cilantro (coriander).

THAI TOM YUM SOUP

Ingredients

2 chicken legs

2 red chili peppers

10 oz / 300 g string beans

4 cups / 1 liter beef broth (stock)

2 kaffir lime leaves

1 stalk lemongrass, slightly crushed

1 tsp freshly grated ginger

1 tsp tamarind concentrate

10 oz / 300 g mini corns

Fish sauce

Chili sauce

Soybean sprouts, to garnish

Method

Prep and cook time: 25 min

1 Remove the skin from the chicken, remove the bone and cut into bite-size pieces.

2 Wash the chili peppers and cut into rings. Wash and trim the string beans.

3 Bring the beef broth (stock), kaffir lime leaves, lemongrass, ginger and tamarind concentrate to a boil. Add the string beans and simmer gently for about 2–3 minutes. Add the chicken, chili and mini corns and simmer for another 5–6 minutes.

4 Season with fish sauce and chili sauce. Remove the lemongrass stick, garnish with the soybean sprouts and serve.

POTATO CURRY SOUP WITH CHICKEN

Ingredients

2–3 large boiling potatoes

2 large carrots

1 onion

2 chicken breasts

2 tbsp oil

1 tbsp curry powder

½ tsp cinnamon

2 tsp garam masala

2½ cups / 600 ml vegetable broth (stock)

1¼ cups / 300 g yogurt

3 tbsp chopped mint leaves

Salt & freshly milled pepper

Method

Prep and cook time: 35 min

1 Peel the potatoes, then rinse and dice. Peel the carrots, cut in half lengthways, then cut diagonally. Peel the onion and cut into slices.

2 Cut the chicken into bite-size pieces and fry in hot oil. Season to taste with salt, pepper and curry powder. Take out of the skillet.

3 Sauté the potatoes, carrots and onions in the meat fat, stirring continually. Season to taste with salt and pepper. Stir in the rest of the spices and pour in the vegetable broth (stock). Simmer gently for about 10 minutes. Add the chicken pieces and simmer for a further 4–5 minutes. Season to taste.

4 Mix the yogurt with 2 tablespoons of chopped mint.

5 Pour the soup into serving bowls and garnish with a spoonful of yogurt sauce and some chopped mint.

HOT AND SOUR SOUP WITH PORK

Ingredients

2 tbsp sesame oil

1 lb / 450 g pork loin, sliced into matchsticks

2 chili peppers, seeded and finely chopped (wear gloves to prevent irritation)

1 inch / 3-cm fresh ginger root, peeled and grated

3½ cups / 800 ml strong chicken broth (stock)

3 tbsp rice vinegar

7 oz / 200 g preserved Mu Err mushrooms, finely sliced*

Soy sauce, to taste

2 tbsp chopped cilantro (fresh coriander) leaves, to garnish

Method

Prep and cook time: 40 min

1 Heat the oil in a skillet or wok. Add the pork and stir-fry until no longer pink, about 1 minute. Transfer to a plate and return the skillet to the heat.

2 Add the ginger and chilies and stir-fry 1 minute, then add the broth (stock), vinegar and mushrooms and simmer for around 20 minutes.

3 Return the pork and its juices to the soup. Season with soy sauce and serve, sprinkled with cilantro (coriander).

*Preserved Mu Err (wood ear) mushrooms can be found in Asian markets. If unavailable substitute sliced fresh shiitake mushrooms.

BOUILLON NIPPON
WITH DUCK BREAST

Ingredients

1 duck breast fillet
(about 10 oz / 300 g)

Salt & freshly milled pepper

1 inch / 3-cm piece fresh ginger

1 chili

6 cups / 1½ liters strong chicken
broth (stock)

1 large carrot

2 scallions (spring onions)

2 oz / 50 g narrow ribbon noodles

2 oz / 60 g small bean sprouts (soybean
or mung bean)

3½ oz / 100 g slice tofu

1 hard-boiled egg

Soy sauce

Method
Prep and cook time: 1 hour

1 Score the skin of the duck breast in a diamond pattern and season with salt and pepper. Then lay in a cold skillet, skin side down, and heat. Turn over as soon as the fat runs. Fry for about 7 minutes, then turn and fry for about a further 7 minutes until crisp. Take out and set aside.

2 Peel and slice the ginger. Wash and deseed the chili. Put the ginger and chili into the broth (stock), cover and simmer for 15 minutes. Strain the broth through a sieve.

3 Peel the carrot and cut into thin strips lengthways (or into shapes using a cutter). Wash and trim the scallions (spring onions) and cut into rings at an angle.

4 Cook the noodles according to the package instructions, drain and refresh in cold water.

5 Rinse the bean sprouts in cold water and drain. Dice the tofu. Shell and slice the egg. Cut the duck breast into thin slices.

6 Divide the noodles, vegetables, tofu, egg and meat between soup bowls, add hot broth and season to taste with soy sauce. Serve at once.

TAMARIND AND COCONUT SOUP

Ingredients

$^1/_3$ cup / 80 ml sesame oil

1 red onion, peeled and chopped

2 cloves garlic, peeled and chopped

1 red chili, chopped

1–2 tsp cumin

1 tsp ground coriander

2 very ripe plantains, peeled and cut into $^1/_2$ inch (1 cm) slices

2$^1/_2$ cups / 600 ml chicken broth (stock)

$^1/_4$ cup / 50 ml tamarind paste

1$^1/_4$ cups / 300 ml unsweetened coconut milk

1 tsp sea salt

$^1/_2$ cup roughly chopped cilantro (coriander) leaves

$^1/_2$ cup roughly chopped fresh mint leaves

Method
Prep and cook time: 35 min

1 Heat the sesame oil in a large pan and add the red onion, garlic, half of the chili, cumin and ground coriander. Sauté for 5 minutes, stirring continuously so it doesn't stick.

2 Add the plantains, broth (stock), tamarind paste and coconut milk and bring to a boil. Turn the heat to a gentle simmer and cook until the plantains are soft, then remove from the heat.

3 Add the salt and purée the soup. Return to the heat and add the rest of the chili.

4 Stir in the cilantro (coriander) and mint just before serving.

SHIITAKE MUSHROOM AND NOODLE SOUP

Ingredients

2 tbsp vegetable oil

1 cup / 125 g sliced shiitake mushrooms

4 scallions (spring onions), trimmed and chopped

1 clove garlic, minced

1 carrot, cut into very thin sticks

¾ cup / 75 g halved snow peas (mangetout)

5 cups / 1.25 liters chicken broth (stock)

2 tbsp light soy sauce

2 tbsp dry sherry

2 oz / 50 g instant or thin rice noodles (vermicelli)

1 cup / 200 g baby corn

Method
Prep and cook time: 20 min

1 Heat the oil in a skillet or wok, then add the mushrooms and stir-fry for 2 minutes.

2 Add the scallions (spring onions), garlic, carrot and snow peas (mangetout) and stir-fry for a further 2 minutes. Pour in the broth (stock), soy sauce and sherry and bring to a boil.

3 Add the rice noodles and baby corn and cook for 3 minutes or until noodles and corn are tender. Serve in bowls.

MISO SOUP WITH VEGETABLES

Ingredients

2 tbsp miso

1 tbsp vegetable broth granules

1 small carrot, peeled and cut into matchsticks

¼ nori sheet, cut into thin strips

1 bunch radishes, trimmed and halved

½ tsp ground ginger

Salt

Method

Prep and cook time: 15 min

1 Put the miso into a pan with 3 tablespoons water and heat until it dissolves. Add 4 cups / 1 liter water and the broth granules.

2 Add the radishes, carrots and ginger to the soup and simmer for about 4 minutes. Season to taste with salt. Divide the nori strips between 4 bowls, ladle the hot soup over them and serve.

CHINESE SOUP
WITH BABY SWEETCORN

Ingredients

5 cups / 1.25 liters chicken broth (stock)

8 Chinese cabbage leaves, shredded

1 cup / 50 g baby spinach leaves

1 cup / 200 g baby corn, sliced lengthwise

1 tbsp light soy sauce

2 tbsp dark soy sauce

2 tbsp rice wine or dry sherry

2 tsp superfine (caster) sugar

2 tsp sesame oil

Salt and freshly ground pepper, to taste

Fresh ginger root, peeled and slivered, to garnish

Method

Prep and cook time: 20 min

1 Bring the chicken broth (stock) to a simmer in a medium saucepan. Add the cabbage, spinach leaves and baby corn and simmer for 3 minutes.

2 Add the light and dark soy sauce, wine or sherry, and sugar and simmer for 5 minutes more.

3 Season with sesame oil, salt and pepper. Ladle into bowls and garnish with slivered ginger.

CHICKEN SOUP
WITH BEAN SPROUTS

Ingredients

For the curry paste:

1 chili

1 shallot

½ tsp chopped lemongrass

1 tsp freshly grated ginger

Good pinch cumin

1 tsp ground curcuma (turmeric)

For the soup:

14 oz / 400 g chicken breast fillet

2 garlic cloves

¾ inch / 2-cm piece of fresh ginger

1 stalk lemongrass

2 tbsp oil

1½ cups / 200 g soybean sprouts

1¾ cups / 400 ml chicken broth (stock)

1¾ cups / 400 ml unsweetened coconut milk

2 tbsp lime juice

2 tbsp fish sauce

Fresh mint leaves, to garnish

Method
Prep and cook time: 30 min

1 Put all the curry paste ingredients into a mortar and grind to a paste.

2 Poach the chicken in simmering salted water for 5–8 minutes. Take out of the water and let drain. Tear the meat into pieces in the direction of the grain.

3 Peel and finely chop the garlic and ginger. Crush the lemongrass. Heat the oil in a wok. Put the meat, ginger, garlic and lemongrass into the wok and fry briefly.

4 Add the bean sprouts and fry briefly then stir in the chicken broth (stock). Add the coconut milk and 1 tablespoon curry paste and bring to a boil.

5 Draw the wok away from the heat and season with lime juice and fish sauce. Remove the lemongrass.

6 Ladle the soup into bowls and serve garnished with mint leaves.

SCALLOP SOUP
WITH CHILI AND LEMONGRASS

Ingredients

1 stick lemongrass

½ red chili

1 inch / 3-cm piece ginger,
freshly grated

4 cups / 1 liter fish broth (stock)

1½ tbsp fish sauce

Salt & freshly milled pepper

1 tbsp lime juice

1 tbsp oil

4 scallops, ready prepared

Basil leaves, to garnish

Cilantro (coriander) leaves, to garnish

Method

Prep and cook time: 25 min

1 Remove the outer leaves from the lemongrass and finely chop. Wash the chili, remove the seeds and cut into rings. Peel the ginger and grate very finely.

2 Bring the fish broth (stock), fish sauce, lemongrass, ginger and chili to a boil and simmer for about 10 minutes. Season to taste with salt, pepper and lime juice.

3 In the meantime, heat the oil in a skillet and fry the scallops for about 1 minute on each side.

4 Put in the hot soup and leave to stand for a while. Season again, then spoon into bowls, garnish with the cilantro (coriander) and basil leaves and serve.

HOT AND SOUR SHRIMP SOUP

Ingredients

12 whole shrimp (or prawns)

7 oz / 200 g straw mushrooms, enoki or white mushrooms

2 chilies

1 stalk lemongrass

4 cups / 1 liter chicken broth (stock)

6 kaffir lime leaves

Juice of 1 lime

1 tsp galangal, freshly grated

Fish sauce

Cilantro (coriander) leaves to garnish

Method

Prep and cook time: 20 min

1 Wash the shrimp (or prawns).

2 Clean the mushrooms.

3 Wash and slice the chilies.

4 Shred the lemongrass very finely.

5 Put the chicken broth (stock) into a pan and bring to a boil. Put all the ingredients into the broth and cook very gently for 6–8 minutes. Add fish sauce to taste and serve scattered with cilantro (coriander).

PUMPKIN SOUP WITH CHICKEN

Ingredients

2 chicken breasts

1–2 tbsp light soy sauce

1 small pumpkin

1 onion

¾ inch / 2-cm piece of fresh ginger

2 tbsp dried jelly ear fungus

2 cups / 500 ml vegetable broth (stock)

1 red chili

1¾ cups / 400 ml coconut milk

2–3 tomatoes

Salt & freshly milled pepper

Thai basil, to garnish

Method

Prep and cook time: 45 min

1 Cut the chicken into strips and marinate in 1–2 tablespoons soy sauce. Peel, deseed and dice the pumpkin. Peel and slice the onion. Peel and finely chop the ginger. Chop the jelly ear fungus and soak in a little hot water.

2 Put the onion, ginger and pumpkin into a pan with the vegetable broth (stock). Slit the chili open lengthways, deseed and add to the pan. Cook for about 20 minutes with a lid on the pan. Then remove the chili and take half of the vegetables out of the broth (stock).

3 Finely purée the rest of the vegetables with the broth. Drain the jelly ear fungus and add to the soup with the coconut milk. Bring to a boil. Boil for 2–3 minutes, then return the vegetables to the soup.

4 Deseed the tomatoes and cut into pieces. Add to the soup with the chicken. Briefly bring to a boil, then cook gently for 7 minutes.

5 Season to taste and ladle into bowls. Serve garnished with basil.

SPICY BEEF SOUP

Ingredients

3½ oz / 100 g ribbon pasta

10 oz / 300 g beef

2 carrots

2 chili peppers

2 red bell peppers

7 oz / 200 g string beans

1 bunch scallions (spring onions)

3¼ cups / 800 ml beef broth (stock)

1 stick lemongrass, slightly crushed

2 kaffir lime leaves

Hot chili sauce

Fish sauce

Method

Prep and cook time: 35 min

1 Cook the pasta in boiling, salted water according to instructions on the packet until al dente. Rinse under cold water, then drain.

2 Cut the beef into thin strips. Peel the carrots and cut into strips. Finely chop the chili peppers, removing the seeds. Cut the bell peppers in half, remove the seeds and cut into strips. Wash the string beans and chop diagonally. Wash the scallions (spring onions) and cut diagonally into rings.

3 Bring the beef broth (stock), lemongrass and kaffir lime leaves to a boil. Add the beans, chili peppers and the carrots and simmer for about 5 minutes. Now add the scallions and the bell pepper and simmer for a further 5 minutes. Add the pasta and the beef for the last 4–5 minutes. Season with chili sauce and fish sauce. Remove the lemongrass and the lime leaves and serve.

CHICKEN LAKSA

Ingredients

For the paste:

2 garlic cloves, peeled

2 tbsp freshly chopped cilantro (coriander)

4 green chili peppers

1 large chopped onion

1 tsp shrimp paste

2 tsp oil

4 chicken breasts, skinned

3½ oz / 100 g thin rice noodles

2 tbsp sesame oil

2 tbsp coconut cream

8 tbsp coconut milk

3¼ cups / 800 ml chicken broth (stock)

Juice of 2 limes

1 large handful bean sprouts

1 large handful choi sum or spinach

2 tbsp soy sauce

4 scallions (spring onions), washed, trimmed and cut into strips

2 limes, cut into wedges

Cilantro (coriander) leaves, to garnish

Method

Prep and cook time: 25 min plus
24 hours marinating time

1 Purée the peeled garlic, chopped cilantro (coriander), chili peppers (minus seeds), onion, oil and shrimp paste.

2 Spread the chicken breasts with about half the paste and marinate in the refrigerator, covered, for about 24 hours.

3 Cut up the noodles with scissors and soak in hot water.

4 Then heat the sesame oil in a frying pan and brown the chicken breasts on both sides. Add the rest of the paste, the coconut cream and milk, the broth (stock), lime juice and soy sauce and simmer for about 8–10 minutes. Add the noodles, bean sprouts and choi sum (or spinach) and cook for about 1 minute.

5 Divide the noodles between 4 bowls, add a little of the sauce and vegetables to each. Then place a chicken breast and the rest of the vegetables on top of each bowl of noodles. Garnish with scallions (spring onions), lime wedges and cilantro (coriander) leaves.

STARTERS AND SALADS

SHRIMP BALLS

Ingredients

2 scallions (spring onions), only the white parts

1 lb 6 oz / 600 g peeled shrimp (or prawns), pre-prepared

1 tsp ginger, grated

2 garlic cloves, finely chopped

1 egg white

1 tbsp cornstarch (cornflour)

Salt

Cayenne pepper

Soy sauce

1 pak choi

Method
Prep and cook time: 30 min

1 Trim the scallions (spring onions), halve lengthwise and chop very finely.

2 Wash the shrimp (or prawns), pat dry and purée half very finely. Finely chop the other half. Combine with the scallions, ginger, garlic and the egg white. If the mixture is too soft, work in some cornstarch (cornflour). Season with salt, a little soy sauce and cayenne pepper and form into about 20 balls with moist hands.

3 Wash the pak choi and arrange loosely on a base of the bamboo steamer. Drizzle with soy sauce. Place the shrimp balls on top and steam over boiling water with the lid on for about 10 minutes.

4 If you wish, serve with chili or soy sauce dip.

STUFFED BANANA LEAVES

Ingredients

1 lb 12 oz / 800 g tofu

Soy sauce

1 lb 2 oz / 500 g mixed ground beef and pork

1 chili, finely chopped

1 tsp grated ginger

1 clove garlic, finely chopped

6 banana leaves, each about 6 x 2 inches / 15 x 5 cm

Toothpicks (cocktail sticks)

Method

Prep and cook time: 25 min plus marinating time 30 min

1 Cut the tofu into 24 cubes and marinate in plenty of soy sauce for about 30 minutes.

2 Mix the ground meat with the chili, ginger and garlic. Season with a little soy sauce and form into 12 balls.

3 Place a meatball in the center of each banana leaf, put a cube of tofu on either side and wrap the banana leaf around them. Secure with toothpicks (cocktail sticks) and cook on all sides on a broiler (grill), or in the oven at 350°F (180°C / Gas Mark 4) for about 8 minutes.

THAI FISH AND SHRIMP ROLLS

Ingredients

10 oz / 300 g fish fillet

5 oz / 150 g peeled shrimp (or prawns)

3 small green chilies

²/₃ cup / 50 g coconut flakes

1 tsp shrimp paste

Salt

Freshly ground pepper

1 tsp cane sugar

12 skewers or 6 lemongrass stalks, halved lengthways

Oil, for frying

For the chili sauce:

1 lb 10 oz / 750 g fully ripe tomatoes

3 red chilies

1 onion

2 tbsp olive oil

2 garlic cloves

1 tbsp tomato paste

1 tbsp vinegar

2½ tbsp sugar

Salt & freshly ground pepper

1 tsp cornflour

Method
Prep and cook time: 1 hour

1 Wash and dry the fish fillet and the shrimp (or prawns). Cut into pieces and mash finely in a blender.

2 Wash, core and finely chop the chili, grind in a mortar with the coconut flakes, shrimp paste, a little salt, pepper and sugar. Then mix smoothly with the ground fish and shrimp mixture.

3 Form the mixture into a thick roll, cut the roll into about 12 equal sized disks and shape the disks into rectangles (about 1 x 3 inches / 3 x 8 cm). Wrap each skewer or lemongrass stalk with a rectangle and roll the dough into a smooth shape around the skewers on a work surface, using lightly oiled hands.

4 Pour oil into a deep pan to a depth of about ½ inch (1 cm) and heat. Fry the skewers in batches over medium heat for about 7 minutes until crispy on all sides. Serve with sweet and sour chili sauce.

5 For the sauce, scald the tomatoes for a few seconds, peel, quarter, core and chop. Finely chop the chilies, removing the seeds and white parts.

6 Peel and chop the onion, sweat in hot oil in a pan together with the chilies. Crush the garlic, add to the pan, mix the tomato paste and the tomatoes as well and leave to sweat for a few minutes. Add the sugar, vinegar, salt and 1 bowl of water, cover with a lid and let simmer for 15 minutes.

7 Mix the cornstarch (cornflour) with 1 tbsp cold water evenly, stir this mixture into the sauce, bring to a boil and let thicken a little bit. Season with salt and pepper.

SPRING ROLLS WITH CHILI DIP

Ingredients

For the filling:

3½ cups / 100 g glass noodles

8 oz / 250 g carrots

8 oz / 250 g white cabbage

1½ cups / 200 g soybean sprouts

3 cloves garlic

4 cups / 1 liter oil, to fry

7 oz / 200 g ground beef or finely chopped shrimp

Salt & freshly milled pepper

2 tsp sugar

1 egg

About 40 spring roll wrappers

1 jar Thai sweet chili dip, to serve

Method
Prep and cook time: 50 min

1 Soak the glass noodles in cold water for 30 minutes.

2 Peel and roughly grate the carrots. Shred the cabbage finely. Rinse the soybean sprouts and drain well. Put all these ingredients into a bowl and mix.

3 Peel and finely chop the garlic. Heat 3 tablespoons of the oil in a skillet or wok and briefly fry the garlic. Add the ground meat and fry for 3–5 minutes, breaking it up until brown all over. Season with salt and pepper and leave to cool slightly.

4 Drain the glass noodles, cut into about 2 inch (4 cm) lengths and add to the vegetables. Season with salt, pepper and a little sugar. Add the cooled ground meat and mix well.

5 Lightly beat the egg. Take 1 spring roll wrapper and place on a work surface. Put about 2 heaped tablespoons of the filling across the middle of the wrapper. Turn in the sides and roll up to make a roll about 4 inches (10 cm) long. Use a little beaten egg to stick the edge of the spring roll. Repeat with the other wrappers.

6 Heat the remaining oil in a wok or skillet. (The oil is hot enough when bubbles form on the handle of a wooden spoon held in the oil.) Fry the spring rolls in batches for about 6–8 minutes until golden brown. Take out, drain on a paper towel and serve with chili dip.

THAI *SAGO BALLS*
WITH PEANUT FILLING

Ingredients

14 oz / 400 g sago

7 oz / 200g can of corn

²/₃ cup / 100 g peanuts

3 garlic cloves

1 onion

3 tbsp oil

1 tsp freshly grated ginger

2 tbsp chopped cilantro (coriander) leaves

2 tbsp soy sauce

Fish sauce

Cayenne pepper

Method

Prep and cook time: 40 min

1 Wash the sago in a sieve with plenty of cold water, then put in a bowl. Pour ½ cup (120 ml) of water into the bowl and knead the sago to a smooth dough. Let rest uncovered.

2 For the filling wash the corn and let drain. Chop the peanuts. Peel and finely chop the garlic. Likewise, peel and finely chop the onion.

3 Gently fry the garlic in hot oil until golden brown and take half of it out of the pan for the garnish.

4 Add the onion to the garlic remaining in the pan, fry until golden brown, then add the ginger, peanuts and corn. Remove from the heat, work in the cilantro (coriander) and soy sauce and season well with fish sauce.

5 Form walnut-sized balls from the sago dough, flatten the balls, fill each one with 1–2 teaspoons. of the mixture and roll the dough back into a ball.

6 Steam for about 15 minutes in a bamboo steamer. Serve garnished with the rest of the garlic.

DEEP-FRIED CORN FRITTERS

Ingredients

14 oz / 400 g can corn kernels

5 oz / 150 g ground pork

2 cloves garlic, peeled

1 tbsp sugar

2 eggs

About 1 tbsp cornstarch (cornflour)

Fish sauce

Cayenne pepper

Oil for deep-frying

Toothpicks (cocktail sticks)

Method
Prep and cook time: 20 min

1 Drain the corn kernels well. Finely purée half of the corn with the ground pork, garlic, sugar, eggs and 1 tablespoon cornstarch (cornflour).

2 Then mix in the rest of the corn kernels and add a little more cornstarch if necessary. Season with fish sauce and cayenne pepper.

3 With damp hands form the mixture into small balls. Heat the oil and fry for 2–3 minutes, turning occasionally, until golden brown.

4 Drain on paper towel and serve speared on toothpicks.

THAI SHRIMP WITH LETTUCE

Ingredients

1 bunch fresh cilantro (coriander)

1 round lettuce

1 garlic clove

2 tbsp sesame oil

1 lb 2 oz / 500 g ready-to-cook shrimp or king prawns, (fresh or frozen)

1 lime, juiced

1 tsp honey

Salt & freshly ground pepper

Method

Prep and cook time: 20 min

1 Wash the cilantro (coriander) and shake dry. Pick off a handful of leaves and chop finely. Wash the lettuce and shake dry.

2 Peel the garlic clove and chop finely.

3 Heat the sesame oil and fry the (thawed) shrimp on both sides for about 2 minutes. Add the cilantro and the garlic and briefly fry together. Add the lime juice and season with salt, honey and pepper.

4 Arrange the salad and the shrimp in dishes. Serve garnished with cilantro.

SPRING ROLLS
WITH CHILI-NUT DIP

Ingredients

For the dip:

1/3 cup / 50 g peanuts

4 tbsp sweet chili sauce

2 tbsp fish sauce

1 tbsp chopped cilantro (coriander) leaves

For the spring rolls:

4 sheets rice paper

2 carrots

14 oz / 400 g can crab meat

1 bunch Thai basil

Method

Prep and cook time: 30 min

1 To make the dip, roughly chop the peanuts and toast in a dry skillet until golden brown.

2 Pour in the chili sauce and fish sauce and stir. Add a little water if necessary. Remove from the heat and let cool. Add the chopped cilantro (coriander).

3 For the spring rolls, soak the rice paper according to instructions on the packet.

4 Peel the carrots and cut into thin strips. Drain the crab meat well. Pick the Thai basil leaves from their stem.

5 Place some of the carrots, crab meat and Thai basil leaves in the center of each rice paper and roll. Cut each in half and serve with the dip.

NAAN BREAD
WITH MANGO CHUTNEY

Ingredients

1/3 cup / 75 ml milk

1/3 oz / 10 g yeast, fresh

2 tsp sugar

2½ cups / 250 g all-purpose (plain) flour

½ tsp salt

½ tsp baking powder

1 tbsp oil

3 oz / 75 g plain yogurt

1 small egg

Oil, for the cookie sheet

1 bunch parsley, chopped

For the mango chutney:

7oz / 200 g mango, peeled and diced

2 tbsp golden raisins (sultanas)

2 tbsp brown sugar

1–2 tbsp red wine vinegar

Salt & freshly milled pepper

1 stick cinnamon

2 cloves

1 bay leaf

1 tbsp paprika

Method

Prep and cook time:
Bread: 30 min plus 1 hour 15 mins rising time
Chutney: 30 min plus cooling time

1 Warm the milk and pour in a bowl. Crumble the yeast over the top and add 1 teaspoon sugar. Stir until dissolved and leave for 15 minutes until frothy.

2 Sift the flour into a large bowl, add the salt and the baking powder and mix. Now add 1 teaspoon sugar, the milk and yeast mixture, the oil, the yogurt and the egg and knead to form a smooth dough. Form a ball, cover and leave in a warm place for about an hour to rise.

3 Oil the cookie sheet and pre-heat the oven to 475°F (230°C / Gas Mark 8).

4 Knead the dough again, together with the chopped parsley and divide into 4 pieces. Make 4 balls, then roll out on a floured surface to a naan form. Place on the cookie sheet and bake in the oven for about 8 minutes until golden brown.

5 To make the mango chutney mix all ingredients together with 3–4 tablespoons water. Bring to a boil, stirring continually, Simmer for 10–15 minutes until the mango is soft. Season to taste, then let cool. Remove the bay leaf, cloves and cinnamon stick.

6 Pour into small bowls and serve together with the fresh naan bread.

SAMOSAS

Ingredients

For the filling:

1 onion, finely chopped

1 cup / 300 g cauliflower florets

1 cup / 100 g frozen green beans, chopped into small pieces

2–3 tbsp ghee or clarified butter

½ tsp cumin seeds

2 tsp freshly grated ginger

½ tsp chili powder

Spices mix: 1 tsp each of coriander, sweet paprika and garam masala

1 cup / 125 g frozen peas

Salt

For the pastry:

3 cups / 300 g all-purpose (plain) flour

4 tbsp ghee or clarified butter

1 tsp salt

Oil for deep frying, plus some for the work surface

Method
Prep and cook time: 1 hour

1 For the pastry, put the flour, ghee or clarified butter, salt and ¾ cup (175 ml) water in a bowl. Mix the ingredients together and knead to a smooth dough. Cover and leave to rest for about 20 minutes.

2 Blanch the cauliflower florets and the beans in boiling, salted water for 4 minutes, then place in cold water and drain.

3 Heat the ghee in a saucepan. Fry the cumin over a medium heat for about 1 minute then add the ginger and all the other spices, apart from the salt, and stir. Add the onions and sauté, then add all the vegetables and fry for about 3 minutes, stirring occasionally. Reduce the heat, cover with a lid and simmer for about 5 minutes in the juices. Season with salt and let cool.

4 Divide the dough into 8 portions. Oil a large, wooden board and roll out each ball to a rectangle 8 x 4 inches (20 x 10 cm) in size. Now cut in half to form a square.

5 Divide the filling between the pastry wrappers and fold each wrapper diagonally in half to form a triangle. Press the edges down firmly.

6 Heat the oil in a large saucepan over a medium heat. Fry the samosas in the hot oil for 3–4 minutes, a few at a time. Turn once. Place the cooked samosas on paper towels to drain. Keep warm until ready to serve.

ONION BHAJIS

Ingredients

2 onions

2 green chilis

½ tsp chili powder

2 tbsp finely chopped cilantro (coriander) leaves

3 tbsp lemon juice

1 tsp cumin seeds, roughly crushed in a mortar

7 tbsp chickpea flour (gram flour)

Pinch of salt

2 tbsp water

Sunflower oil, for deep-frying

Method

Prep and cook time: 40 min

1 Peel the onions and slice into very thin rings. Wash the chilis, slit open lengthways, remove the seeds and white inner ribs and finely dice the flesh. Mix both with the chili powder, cilantro (coriander), lemon juice and cumin.

2 Stir the chickpea flour and salt into the onion mixture. Add the water and mix well.

3 Heat the oil in a pan (it is hot enough when bubbles form on the handle of a wooden spoon held in the oil). Take small balls of the onion mixture with a teaspoon and fry in the hot oil, a few at a time, until golden. Drain on a paper towel and keep warm in the oven at the lowest heat. When all the bhajis are cooked, serve at once.

DICED SALMON WITH SOY DIP

Ingredients

1 lb 2 oz / 500 g salmon fillets, without skin, cut into bite-size cubes

For the marinade:

2 lemons, juice and zest

1 tbsp whole grain mustard

1 tbsp olive oil

For the dip:

1 red chili

1 scallion (spring onion)

5 tbsp light soy sauce

1 tbsp chopped cilantro (coriander) leaves

Salt and freshly ground pepper

Method

Prep and cook time: 20 min plus 30 min marinating time

1 Mix together all ingredients for the marinade and marinate the salmon cubes for about 30 minutes.

2 Remove the salmon from the marinade and place under a hot broiler (grill) for 2–3 minutes until lightly browned. Brush with marinade from time to time.

3 For the dip, de-seed and finely chop the chili. Trim the scallion (spring onion) and cut into rings.

4 Mix all the dip ingredients and season to taste. Serve the salmon with the dip.

SHRIMP CAKES
WITH SWEET-AND-SOUR
SAUCE

Ingredients

1¾ lb / 800 g shrimp (prawns),
peeled and de-veined

1 small hot chili pepper

3 cloves garlic, chopped

2 sprigs cilantro (fresh coriander)

½ tsp salt

Freshly ground pepper, to taste

1 egg

Neutral-tasting vegetable oil for frying

Sweet-and-sour sauce, for dipping

Method
Prep and cook time: 20 min

1 Finely chop the shrimp (prawns). Wearing gloves
to prevent irritation, seed and devein the chili and
finely chop. Crush the chili, garlic and cilantro
(coriander) leaves in a mortar with the salt and
pepper. Add the shrimp and blend to a paste. Add
the egg and mix well.

2 Form the mixture into approximately 2-inch
(5 cm) patties, using about 2 tablespoons of the
mixture for each one.

3 In a large skillet, heat the oil and fry the shrimp
cakes for about 2 minutes, until golden brown.
Drain on paper towels. Serve at once with the
sweet-and-sour sauce.

SPICY NOODLE SALAD

Ingredients

1 carrot

1 cucumber

2 shallots

½ cup /50 g bean sprouts

3 red chilis

7 oz / 200 g rice noodles

Cilantro (coriander) and mint leaves, shredded

For the Nuoc Cham Sauce:

5 cloves garlic, chopped very finely

5 red chilis, deseeded and very finely chopped

3½ tbsp Vietnamese fish sauce

Scant ½ cup / 100 ml water

3½ tbsp rice vinegar

¼ cup / 50 g sugar

Juice of 1 large lemon

Method

Prep and cook time: 25 min

1 Peel and halve the carrot and cucumber. Remove the cucumber seeds, cut the cucumber in half and cut lengthways into long, very thin strips. Cut the carrot into long very thin sticks. Peel the shallots and slice thinly. Wash and drain the soybean sprouts. Halve and deseed the chilis and cut into rings. Reserve a couple of chili rings to garnish.

2 Cook the noodles in boiling, salted water for about 2 minutes. Then drain, refresh in cold water and drain thoroughly. Set aside.

3 For the sauce, put all the ingredients apart from the lemon juice into a pan and heat, but do not let it boil. Then remove from heat and let cool. Stir in the lemon juice when the sauce is cold.

4 Put the noodles, cucumber, carrots, shallots, chilies and 6 tbsp of Nuoc Cham sauce into a large bowl and mix. Serve sprinkled with herbs and the reserved chili rings.

SWEET AND SOUR CHICKEN SALAD

Ingredients

For the dressing:

2 tbsp honey

4 tbsp olive oil

Finely grated zest and juice of 1 orange

2 tbsp sweet chili sauce

Salt and freshly ground pepper, to taste

For the salad:

4 cooked smoked chicken breasts, cut into chunks

2 cups / 400 g drained canned or thawed frozen corn kernels

1 cucumber, cut into bite-size chunks

1 clementine / mandarin orange, peeled and segmented

1 large carrot, sliced into matchsticks

5 oz / 150 g mixed salad greens

To garnish:

Deep fried rice noodles (rice sticks)

Method

Prep and cook time: 25 min

1 To make the dressing spoon the honey into a small jar with a tightly fitting lid. Add the oil, orange zest and juice and sweet chili sauce. Season with salt and ground black pepper and shake to mix.

2 Place the chicken, corn, cucumber, clementine (mandarin orange), carrots and salad leaves into large bowl. Toss together.

3 Drizzle with the dressing and garnish with the rice noodles.

WAKAME, WATER CHESTNUT AND ORANGE SALAD

Ingredients

¾ oz / 20 g dried wakame seaweed

1 cucumber, seeded and cut into thin strips

1½ cups / 150 g snow peas (mangetout) cut into thin strips

1 inch / 3-cm piece fresh ginger root, peeled and finely grated

1 cup / 200 g canned sliced water chestnuts, drained

2 oranges

5 tbsp rice vinegar

1 tbsp sugar

½ tsp light soy sauce

Pinch salt

To garnish:

1 red chili pepper, seeded and finely chopped (wear gloves to prevent irritation)

4 tsp sesame seeds

Method

Prep and cook time: 1 hour

1 Put the wakame into a bowl and add enough warm water to cover. Soak until softened, about15 minutes.

2 Put the cucumber in a colander and sprinkle with about 1 tsp salt. Leave for 10 minutes to soften.

3 Drain the wakame, cut off and discard any hard spines and chop lengthwise. Return to the bowl and add the snow peas (mangetout), ginger and water chestnuts.

4 Use a small sharp knife or vegetable peeler to remove orange peel, scraping off all traces of white pith. Remove the flesh from the orange membranes, catching and reserving any juice. Halve the orange segments and add to the bowl along with the juice.

5 Rinse the cucumber and squeeze out the excess water; add to the salad bowl.

6 To prepare the dressing, put the sugar, rice vinegar and soy sauce into a small jar with a tight-fitting lid; add the salt and shake to blend. Drizzle over the salad and leave to marinate for 30 minutes.

7 Garnish with some chopped red chili and serve with a sprinkling of sesame seeds.

NOODLE SALAD WITH SHRIMP

Ingredients

7 oz / 200 g cellophane noodles

2 tbsp vegetable oil, divided

8 jumbo shrimp (king prawns)

1–2 cloves garlic, minced

2 tbsp lime juice, divided

2 eggs, beaten

½ cup / 50 g bean sprouts

1–2 scallions (spring onions), chopped into 2-inch (5-cm) pieces (reserve a few for garnish)

¼ cup chopped roasted peanuts

4 slices pickled red ginger, chopped

1–2 tbsp rice vinegar

Fish sauce, to taste

Chili sauce, to taste

Salt and white pepper, to taste

Method

Prep and cook time: 40 min

1 Put the cellophane noodles into a bowl, pour plenty of boiling water over them and let stand until softened, 10 minutes. Drain. Cut the noodles into smaller lengths.

2 Heat 1 tablespoon of the oil in a wok or skillet and quickly stir-fry the shrimp (prawns) and garlic. Sprinkle with 1 tablespoon lime juice and set aside.

3 Heat the rest of the oil in a small skillet and scramble the eggs.

4 Mix the cellophane noodles with the bean sprouts, scallions (spring onions), scrambled eggs, peanuts and ginger. Divide onto plates.

5 In a small bowl whisk the rice vinegar, the rest of the lime juice, fish sauce, chili sauce, salt and white pepper; sprinkle over the salad. Put the shrimp on top of the salad and garnish with the reserved slivered scallions.

CHICKEN SALAD
WITH MINT LEAVES

Ingredients

For the curry paste:

2 chilies

1 shallot

½ tsp freshly gated ginger

1 tsp shrimp paste

For the salad:

1 bunch scallions
(spring onions)

12 oz / 400 g mixed
salad leaves

1 handful mint leaves

1 handful cilantro
(coriander) leaves

1 onion

2 tomatoes

1 lb / 450 g chicken legs,
skinned and boned

1 tsp finely grated lemongrass

2 tbsp oil

For the dressing:

1 tbsp brown sugar

2 tbsp fish sauce

2 tbsp lime juice

Lemongrass, finely shredded
lengthways, to garnish

Cilantro (coriander) leaves,
to garnish

Mint leaves, to garnish

Method
Prep and cook time: 30 min

1 Put all the curry paste ingredients into a
mortar and grind to a paste.

2 Trim the scallions (spring onions) and cut into
rings. Put the salad leaves into a bowl with the
roughly chopped herbs and scallions (spring
onions). Mix. Peel and dice the onion. Cut the
tomatoes into wedges.

3 Cut the chicken into strips and put into a
bowl with 2 tablespoons of the curry paste and

the lemongrass. Mix. Heat the oil, brown the
meat on all sides then stir-fry for about
2 minutes. Take out of the skillet and sauté
the diced onion in the oil.

4 Add the tomatoes and fry briefly, then return
the meat to the skillet and cook gently until
cooked through. Put the chicken, tomatoes and
onion on top of the salad.

5 Heat the sugar, fish sauce and lime juice
in the skillet. Drizzle over the salad. Serve
garnished with lemongrass and herbs.

SALAD WITH SHRIMP AND PEANUTS

Ingredients

7 oz / 200 g shrimp (or prawns), ready-prepared

1 fresh red chili pepper

2–3 garlic cloves

1 piece of ginger, about
1½ inches/4cms long

4 tbsp peanuts, chopped

4 tbsp oil

²/₃ cup / 150 ml fish broth (stock)

Salt & freshly milled pepper

2 good pinches chili powder

2 tbsp soy sauce

1 tbsp oyster sauce

1 lime, juiced

½ bunch cilantro (coriander)

2 cups / 200 g glass noodles

Method

Prep and cook time: 25 min

1 Deseed the chili pepper and finely chop. Peel and finely chop the garlic and ginger. Toast the peanuts in a dry skillet, then place on one side.

2 Heat the oil and gently cook the chilli, garlic and ginger for 3- 4 minutes until softened.

3 Increase the heat and add the shrimp, then pour in the fish broth (stock) and simmer for about 4 minutes. Season with salt, pepper, chili powder, soy sauce, oyster sauce and the juice from 1 lime.

4 Wash the cilantro (coriander), shake dry and roughly chop.

5 Pour boiling water over the glass noodles and leave for about 6 minutes. Drain, rinse with boiling hot water and drain again. Stir the noodles into the shrimp sauce. Add the roughly chopped cilantro.

6 Garnish with toasted peanuts and serve.

ROAST BEEF SALAD

Ingredients

1 lb 6 oz / 600 g well hung beef sirloin

1 tbsp clarified butter or oil

Salt & freshly ground pepper

8 oz / 200 g mixed salad leaves

4 small tomatoes

1 red onion

1 bunch cilantro (coriander) leaves

For the dressing:

2 tbsp white wine vinegar

1 tsp raspberry vinegar

4 tbsp olive oil

1 tsp cane sugar

½ tsp mustard

Salt

About ¼ tsp chili powder

Orange zest, to garnish

Method

Prep and cook time: 50 min

1 Preheat the oven to 325°F (160°C / Gas Mark 3). Trim the beef. Heat the clarified butter in an ovenproof skillet and brown the meat on both sides over a very high heat. Season with salt and pepper, place in a roasting dish and roast in the oven for 20–30 minutes (depending how well-done you like your meat). Take out and let rest for 5 minutes before carving.

2 Quarter the tomatoes. Peel the onion and cut into wedges. Put the salad leaves, tomato, onion and cilantro (coriander) leaves into a bowl. Reserve some cilantro leaves for garnishing.

3 For the dressing, mix all the dressing ingredients, check the seasoning, add to the prepared salad ingredients and toss.

4 Slice the roast beef thinly. Divide the salad between 4 plates and arrange the beef on top.

5 Serve garnished with cilantro leaves and orange zest.

ROAST DUCK SALAD

Ingredients

2 duck breasts, each about
14 oz / 400 g

1 tbsp clarified butter or oil

4 scallions (spring onions)

2 red chilies

14 oz / 400 g string beans

14 oz / 400 g sugarsnap peas

4 tbsp plum sauce

2 tbsp white wine vinegar

2 tbsp lime juice

Salt & freshly milled pepper

½ bunch basil, for garnish

Method

Prep and cook time: 40 min

1 Wash the duck breasts, pat dry, season with salt and pepper and fry in the hot clarified butter. Fry on the skin side for about 10 minutes and on the other side for about 8 minutes. Take out of the skillet, wrap in aluminum foil and leave for about 10 minutes to rest.

2 Wash the scallions (spring onions). Cut the white end into thin rings, the green end into slightly thicker rings. Wash the chilies, remove the seeds and finely chop. Wash and trim the string beans and the sugarsnap peas and blanch them in boiling, salted water for about 4–5 minutes.

3 Take the duck breasts out of the foil, carefully cut off the skin and cut the meat into thin slices. Arrange on 4 pre-warmed plates together with the vegetables and herbs.

4 Mix the plum sauce with the vinegar and the lime juice, drizzle over the salad and serve with freshly milled pepper, and garnished with basil leaves.

FRIED FISH ON MANGO SALAD

Ingredients

4 sea bass fillets, each weighing about 5 oz / 150 g

2 green mangos

1 shallot

2 red Thai chilies

Juice of ½ a lime

1 tbsp brown sugar

Fish sauce

⅓ cup / 50 g peanuts, chopped

2 tbsp flour

Oil for deep-frying

Method

Prep and cook time: 45 min

1 Peel the mangos, cut the flesh away from the stone and shred. Peel and finely dice the shallot. Wash the chili, halve lengthways, remove the seeds and shred the flesh. Mix the mango with the shallot, chili, lime juice and brown sugar. Add fish sauce to taste and let the salad stand for about 20 minutes.

2 Toast the chopped peanuts in a dry frying pan until golden brown.

3 Wash the fish fillets, pat dry and dust with flour. Heat the oil and fry the fish fillets for 3–4 minutes, or until nicely cooked. Drain on paper towel.

4 Put the salad on plates, place a piece of fish on top of each serving of salad and serve sprinkled with peanuts.

GLASS NOODLES WITH CHICKEN

Ingredients

2 cups / 200 g glass noodles

3 or 4 kaffir lime leaves

12 oz / 350 g chicken breast fillet

2 scallions (spring onions)

2 inches / 5 cm ginger, finely chopped

1 or 2 cloves garlic, finely chopped

3 or 4 shallots, finely chopped

2 red chilis, deseeded and finely chopped (wear gloves)

2 tbsp sesame oil

2 tbsp brown sugar

Juice of 2 limes

Salt & pepper

1 small cucumber, peeled and thinly sliced

2 handfuls herbs (e.g. mint, cilantro (coriander), Thai basil)

To garnish:

2 limes, halved

1/3 cup / 50 g unsalted peanuts, roasted

Method

Prep and cook time: 40 min

1 Soak the glass noodles in lukewarm water and cut into smaller lengths with scissors. In a small pan heat about 4 cups (1 liter) water with the kaffir lime leaves and 1 teaspoon salt. Add the chicken breast and simmer gently over a low heat until cooked (and 12–15 minutes). Drain, let the meat cool slightly, then tear into small pieces.

2 Drain the glass noodles and cook in salted water, then refresh in cold water and drain well. Peel and shred the scallions (spring onions). Soak in cold water.

3 Heat the oil in a skillet and sauté the ginger, garlic, shallots and chilis for 2–3 minutes. Stir in the sugar, sauté briefly, then add the glass noodles, chicken and lime juice. Season with pepper, mix well and set aside.

4 Drain the scallions and mix them into the chicken and noodles along with the cucumber and herbs. Pile the salad on plates and serve garnished with lime halves and scattered with peanuts.

MAIN DISHES: MEAT AND POULTY

CHICKEN CURRY
WITH TOMATOES

Ingredients

3–4 chicken breast fillets
(1 lb 6 oz / 600 g)

2 tbsp sesame oil

2 cloves garlic, chopped

1 tsp freshly chopped ginger

Scant 1 cup / 200 ml unsweetened coconut milk

1 tbsp tomato paste (tomato purée)

2 tsp red curry paste

Scant ½ cup / 100 ml vegetable broth (stock)

1 lb 2 oz / 500 g tomatoes

2 sprigs Thai basil

2 sprigs cilantro (coriander)

Salt & freshly milled pepper

Juice of ½ lemon

Method

Prep and cook time: 30 min

1 Cut the chicken breast fillets into strips approximately ½–¾ inches (1.5–2 cm) wide.

2 Heat the sesame oil in a wok or skillet and fry the chicken, garlic and ginger for 3–4 minutes.

3 Then stir in the coconut milk, tomato paste (tomato purée), curry paste and vegetable broth (stock) and simmer for a further 5 minutes or so.

4 Drop the tomatoes into boiling water for a few seconds, refresh in cold water, then skin, quarter, deseed and cut into wedges. Add to the chicken curry shortly before the end of cooking time.

5 To serve, roughly chop the basil and cilantro (coriander) leaves and stir into the curry. Season with salt and pepper and add lemon juice to taste. Serve in bowls accompanied by rice.

SWEET AND SOUR PORK

Ingredients

1 tbsp rice wine

1 tbsp light soy sauce

2 tsp sesame oil

1 lb / 450 g pork loin, cut into cubes

1 egg, lightly beaten

4 tbsp cornstarch (cornflour), divided

Vegetable oil for deep-frying

For the sauce:

1 large carrot, sliced diagonally

2/3 cup / 150 ml chicken broth (stock)

1 tbsp light soy sauce

2 tsp dark soy sauce

2 tsp sesame oil

4 tsp rice vinegar

1 tbsp sugar

2 tbsp ketchup

2 tsp cornstarch (cornflour), mixed to a smooth paste in 1 tbsp water

1 red bell pepper, chopped into diamonds

4 scallions (spring onions), trimmed and roughly chopped

To garnish:

Cilantro (fresh coriander) leaves

Method
Prep and cook time: 40 min

1 Combine the rice wine, soy sauce and sesame oil in a medium bowl; add the pork and toss to coat. Let marinate for 15 minutes.

2 In a wide shallow bowl, beat the egg with 1 tbsp of the cornstarch (cornflour). Place the remaining 3 tbsp cornstarch in another wide shallow bowl.

3 Heat the oil in a deep fat fryer to 180°C / 350°F.

4 Lift the pork from the marinade and toss in the cornstarch to dredge. Then dip the pork into the egg-cornstarch mixture to coat.

5 Working in batches, deep-fry the pork for about 5 minutes or until golden. Drain on paper towels and keep warm.

6 For the sauce, cook the carrot in boiling water until softened, 2 minutes; drain and set aside.

7 In a large skillet or wok, combine the chicken broth (stock), light and dark soy sauce, sesame oil, rice vinegar, sugar, ketchup, and cornstarch and water mixture into a pan and bring to a boil. Cook, stirring, until slightly thickened.

8 Stir in the carrot, pepper and scallions (spring onions).

9 Add the fried pork and heat through, stirring gently. Serve at once, garnished with cilantro (coriander) leaves.

CHICKEN KORMA

Ingredients

1 lb 2 oz / 500 g chicken breast fillet

1 sachet saffron

Good ¾ cup / 200 g plain yogurt

For the spice mixture:

2 onions

3 garlic cloves

2 red chilis

1 tsp freshly grated ginger

½ cup / 50 g ground almonds

In addition:

2 tbsp ghee or clarified butter

A good pinch of ground cardamom

½ tsp ground cinnamon

1½ tsp ground cumin

1½ tsp ground coriander

1–2 lime leaves

2 curry leaves

1¾ cups / 400 ml unsweetened coconut milk

Salt

Sugar

2 tbsp chopped almonds

Chopped celery, to garnish

Method

Prep and cook time: 1 hour plus 4 hours to marinate

1 Cut the chicken into bite-size pieces. Dissolve the saffron in 1 tablespoon hot water and mix with the yogurt. Add the chicken pieces and marinate for about 4 hours.

2 Peel and finely chop the onions and garlic. Wash and trim the chilis, removing the seeds if you wish, and cut into rings. Mix together the onions, garlic, chilis, grated ginger and ground almonds.

3 Melt the ghee or clarified butter in a pan, add the cardamom, cinnamon, cumin and coriander and sauté briefly. Then add the prepared onion and spice mixture, the lime leaves and curry leaves and sauté, stirring, for 2–3 minutes. Now add the coconut milk and the meat with the marinade and cook for about 45 minutes. Season with salt and sugar, stir in the chopped almonds and spoon into bowls.

4 Serve sprinkled with chopped celery.

DAN DAN NOODLES

Ingredients

For the meat topping:

1 tbsp vegetable oil

3 dried chilis, halved (discard seeds)

½ tsp whole Sichuan peppercorns

2 tbsp / 25 g Sichuan ya cai or preserved mustard leaves*

4 oz / 100 g ground beef

2 tsp light soy sauce

Salt, to taste

12 oz / 350 g dried wide Chinese noodles or fettuccini

For the sauce:

1 tsp ground roasted Sichuan peppercorns

1 tbsp light soy sauce

1 tbsp dark soy sauce

2 tbsp chili oil

To garnish:

1 scallion (spring onion), finely chopped

Method

Prep and cook time: 30 min

1 For the meat topping, heat the oil in a wok or skillet over a medium heat. Add the chilies and Sichuan peppercorns and stir-fry for 30 seconds. Add the ya cai or preserved mustard leaves and continue to stir-fry for 2 minutes.

2 Add the beef and cook, stirring, for 10 minutes until the meat is browned all over. Splash in the soy sauce and stir-fry until the meat is a little crisp. Season with salt and keep warm.

3 Bring a pot of salted water to a boil. Add the noodles and cook until tender, 4 minutes.

4 Meanwhile, in a small bowl, combine the roasted Sichuan peppercorns, light and dark soy sauce and chili oil to make a sauce.

5 Drain the noodles. Divide the meat between 4 bowls, top with the noodles and drizzle the sauce over each. Garnish with the chopped scallion (spring onion).

*Look for ya cai (preserved vegetable, usually mustard leaves) in Asian markets. If unavailable, just omit it from the recipe.

BEEF WITH BLACK BEANS

Ingredients

3 tbsp toasted sesame oil, divided

8 shallots, quartered

2 inch / 5-cm piece fresh ginger root, peeled and thinly sliced

2 cloves garlic, thinly sliced

1 head broccoli, stems peeled and cut into small florets

2 heads bok choy, quartered lengthwise

12 oz / 300 g rump steak, thinly sliced and threaded onto skewers

Generous 1/2 cup / 150 g black bean stir-fry sauce

Method

Prep and cook time: 20 min

1 Heat 2 tablespoons of the oil in a large skillet over medium heat. Add the shallots, ginger and garlic and stir-fry for 2 minutes or until just beginning to color.

2 Add the broccoli and bok choy and stir-fry for 2–3 minutes until wilted, but still crisp. Divide between 4 plates or bowls and keep warm.

3 Heat the remaining tablespoon oil in the skillet over high heat. Add the steak skewers and cook, turning occasionally, for 2 minutes or until well browned and cooked to your liking. Reduce the heat.

4 Pour the black bean sauce over the top and add 5 tablespoons of cold water. Cook, stirring gently for 1 minute until the beef is well coated and the sauce is hot. Spoon over the vegetables and serve immediately.

CHICKEN CHOW MEIN

Ingredients

For the noodles:

8 oz / 225 g dried egg noodles

1 tbsp sesame oil

For the chicken and marinade:

2 tsp light soy sauce

2 tsp rice wine or dry sherry

1 tsp sesame oil

½ tsp salt

½ tsp freshly ground
white pepper

4 oz / 100 g skinless boneless
chicken breast, cut into
matchsticks

For the stir-fry:

3 tbsp vegetable oil, divided

1 tbsp minced garlic

½ cup / 50 g snow peas or
sugar snap peas, thinly sliced
lengthwise

⅓ cup / 50 g shredded
cooked ham

2 tsp light soy sauce

2 tsp dark soy sauce

1 tbsp rice wine or dry sherry

1 tsp salt

½ tsp freshly ground pepper

½ tsp sugar

3 tbsp scallions (spring onions),
chopped

1 tsp sesame oil

Method
Prep and cook time: 40 min

1 Cook the noodles in a large pot of boiling water for 3–5 minutes, then drain and refresh in cold water. Toss with the sesame oil and set aside.

2 Combine the soy sauce, rice wine or sherry, sesame oil, salt and white pepper in a medium bowl; add the chicken and toss to coat. Let stand 10 minutes to marinate.

3 Heat a skillet or wok over high heat. Add 1 tablespoon of the vegetable oil and when very hot and slightly smoking, add the shredded chicken. Stir-fry for about 2 minutes, then transfer to a plate.

4 Return the wok to the heat, then add the remaining 2 tablespoons vegetable oil. When slightly smoking, add the garlic and stir-fry for 10 seconds. Then add the snow peas or sugar snaps and ham and stir-fry for about 1 minute.

5 Add the chicken with its juices and the light and dark soy sauce; stir-fry for 3–4 minutes until chicken is nearly cooked. Add the rice wine or sherry, salt, pepper, sugar and scallions. Stir-fry for 2 minutes.

6 Add the noodles and sesame oil and give the mixture a few final stirs to reheat. Turn onto a warm platter and serve at once.

PORK SATAY

Ingredients

For the satay:

1 lb 6 oz / 600 g pork, such as escalopes

2 cloves garlic

1 chili, finely chopped

1 shallot, finely chopped

¼ tsp ground cumin

¼ tsp ground coriander

2 tbsp soy sauce

4 tbsp coconut milk

2 tbsp oil

Salt & freshly ground pepper

Wooden skewers

For the peanut sauce:

1 cup / 150 g unsalted, shelled peanuts

1 dried red chili

4 tbsp oil

1 shallot, chopped

2 tbsp peanut butter

1 tsp curry powder

1 lemon, juice and grated peel

Pinch of sugar

Salt & freshly ground pepper

⅓ cup / 80 ml chicken broth (stock)

Method

Prep and cook time: 25 min plus marinating time 2 hours

1 Cut the pork into thin strips about ¾ inch (2 cm) wide.

2 Mix the rest of the ingredients to make a marinade and marinate the strips of pork for at least 2 hours.

3 Meanwhile make the sauce, toast the peanuts in a dry skillet, leave to cool, then crush finely in a mortar with the chili.

4 Heat the oil and sauté the shallot until translucent. Stir in the peanut butter, curry powder, crushed peanuts and chili, lemon juice and peel, and add sugar, salt and pepper to taste. Then stir in enough chicken broth (stock) to produce a creamy sauce.

5 Then take out of the marinade, drain and thread lengthways on wooden skewers. Grill on a hot grill for about 4 minutes, turning frequently (or fry in oil in a skillet). Serve with the peanut sauce.

SESAME CHICKEN WITH CASHEWS AND VEGETABLES

Ingredients

1 egg white

2 tsp cornstarch (cornflour)

½ tsp salt

4 skinless boneless chicken breasts

2 tbsp vegetable oil, divided

1 tbsp black sesame seeds

2 tsp dark soy sauce

2 tsp cider vinegar

2 tsp chili bean sauce

1 tbsp sesame oil

2 tsp sugar

1 tbsp rice wine or dry sherry

4 scallions (spring onions),
roughly chopped

1 red bell pepper, sliced

1 cup / 200 g baby corn,
cut into bite-size pieces

4 tbsp cashew nuts

Method

Prep and cook time: 45 min

1 In a medium bowl, whisk together the egg white, cornstarch and salt. Add the chicken and stir to coat. Refrigerate for 15 minutes.

2 Meanwhile, to prepare the sauce, heat 1 tbsp of the vegetable oil in a small skillet. Add the sesame seeds and stir-fry for 30 seconds until fragrant. Stir in the soy sauce, cider vinegar, chili bean sauce, sesame oil, sugar and rice wine or dry sherry. Bring to a boil, then remove from the heat and set aside.

3 Bring 1½ cups / 350 ml water to a boil in a large skillet or wok. Add the chicken, reduce the heat and simmer until cooked through, about 4 minutes. Drain, discarding the water. Add the cooked chicken to the sauce and warm through.

4 Return the skillet to the heat and add the remaining tablespoon vegetable oil. Add the scallions (spring onion), red bell pepper, corn and cashews and stir-fry until the vegetables are softened, 3–5 minutes.

5 Divide the vegetable mixture into 4 bowls. Cut each chicken breast into 5 slices and arrange on top of the vegetables. Drizzle with the sesame sauce and serve at once.

GREEN CHICKEN CURRY

Ingredients

For the green curry paste:

1 bunch scallions (spring onions), washed and trimmed

3 medium-size green chilis, de-seeded and roughly chopped

2 garlic cloves, peeled

2 tsp freshly chopped ginger

2 tsp coriander seeds, crushed

Salt & freshly milled pepper

2 stalks lemongrass, peeled and finely chopped

½ bunch basil

1 bunch cilantro (coriander)

3 tbsp olive oil

2 untreated lemons, zest and juice

4 chicken breasts

Oil for frying

1¾ cups / 400 ml unsweetened coconut milk

2 tbsp pistachios, chopped

Method

Prep and cook time: 30 min plus 30 min to marinate

1 Place all ingredients for the green curry paste in a blender and process to a smooth paste.

2 Cut the chicken breasts into 2–3-cm (1-inch) pieces and marinate for about 30 minutes with some of the curry paste. Remove from the marinade and fry in a hot wok in oil for about 4 minutes. Pour in the coconut milk and add the remaining curry paste. Bring to a boil, then simmer gently for 4–5 minutes. Season to taste.

3 Serve with chopped pistachios.

TURKEY WITH COCONUT SAUCE

Ingredients

1 lb 2 oz / 500 g turkey breast fillets

3 tbsp sesame oil

2 garlic cloves, diced

1 onion, diced

2 tsp freshly grated ginger

1 red chili, deseeded and shredded

Juice and zest of ½ a lime

3¼ cups / 800 ml coconut milk

1⅓ cup / 200 g frozen peas

Salt

Brown sugar

Soy sauce

Cilantro (coriander) leaves, to garnish

Method

Prep and cook time: 30 min

1 Slice the turkey into short, narrow strips.

2 Heat 2 tablespoons of sesame oil in a wok or a large skillet. Add the garlic, diced onion, grated ginger, chili and lime peel and sauté briefly.

3 Add the coconut milk and cook for about 10 minutes over a low heat until reduced slightly. Add the frozen peas after about 5 minutes. At the end of the 10 minutes add the turkey and cook very gently in the sauce for a few minutes until the meat is done. Add salt, sugar, lime juice and soy sauce to taste.

4 Serve the turkey with rice and garnish with cilantro (coriander).

CHICKEN JALFREZI

Ingredients

1 lb 2 oz / 500 g chicken breast fillets

1 tbsp Worcestershire sauce

3 onions

7 oz / 200 g sugarsnap peas

1 cup / 150 g frozen peas

2 red chilis, or more according to taste

3 tbsp oil

A good pinch of brown mustard seeds

A good pinch of cumin seeds

A good pinch of ground cumin

A pinch of ground coriander

A good pinch of ground curcuma (turmeric)

2/3–3/4 cup / 150–200 ml coconut cream, to taste

Salt & freshly milled pepper

Mint leaves

Method

Prep and cook time: 25 min

1 Cut the meat into thin strips and mix with the Worcestershire sauce. Peel and slice the onions. Wash and trim the sugarsnap peas. Thaw the frozen peas. Slit the chilis open lengthways, remove the seeds and inner ribs, and finely chop the flesh.

2 Heat the oil in a skillet and fry the mustard seeds and cumin seeds, stirring, for about 30 seconds, until they start to pop. Add the onions and chilis and fry, stirring, until the onions are lightly browned.

3 Stir in the meat, ground spices, Worcestershire sauce, sugarsnap peas and thawed frozen peas and season with salt and pepper. Add 1 cup of water, bring to a boil and cook over a medium heat for a further 3–5 minutes, stirring, until the meat and vegetables are just cooked.

4 Add coconut cream to taste. Sprinkle with mint and serve with rice.

LAMB ROGAN JOSH

Ingredients

6 tbsp oil

8 cardamom seeds

1 inch / 2.5 cm cinnamon stick

2 bay leaves

1 lb 12 oz / 800 g lamb, from the leg, cut into bite-size pieces

6 garlic cloves, peeled and crushed

1 tsp freshly grated ginger

2 onions, chopped

1–2 tsp cumin

1–2 tsp ground coriander

½ tsp cayenne pepper, according to taste

1 tbsp sweet paprika

1–2 tbsp tomato paste (purée)

Salt

Method

Prep and cook time: 1 hour 20 min

1 Heat the oil in a large skillet. Fry the cardamom, cinnamon and bay leaves in the oil, then add the meat und fry until browned on all sides.

2 Take the meat out of the skillet and fry the onions. Mix the garlic with the freshly grated ginger and add the mixture to the onions. Now add the cumin, coriander, cayenne pepper, paprika and tomato paste (purée) and stir. Add the meat, season to taste with salt and pour in 1¼ cups /300 ml water.

3 Bring to a boil and simmer gently for about 1 hour. Serve with rice.

PORK RIBS WITH SCALLIONS AND CHILIES

Ingredients

3 lb 4 oz / 1.5 kg pork ribs (ask your butcher to chop into separate ribs)

Finely grated zest and juice of 2 oranges

3 tbsp soy sauce

2 tbsp tomato paste

2 tbsp vegetable oil

2 tbsp honey

1 inch / 3-cm piece fresh ginger root, peeled and grated

6 mild red chili peppers, slit open lengthwise and seeded

4 scallions (spring onions) green parts only; chopped into 2 inch / 5-cm strips

Method

Prep and cook time: 1 h 20 min plus 2 hours to marinate

1 Bring a large pot of water to a boil. Place the ribs in the boiling water, reduce the heat and simmer until tender, around 45 minutes.

2 To prepare the marinade, in a small bowl, combine the orange zest and juice with the soy sauce, tomato paste, oil, honey and ginger.

3 Remove the ribs from the water and drain. Place in a shallow dish, pour over the marinade mixture and toss to coat well. Cover and marinate for at least 2 hours in the refrigerator.

4 Preheat the broiler (grill); line a broiler pan with foil and place the ribs on the broiler rack. Drizzle with the marinade and broil (grill) for around 10 minutes, until slightly crisped at the edges.

5 Turn the ribs, sprinkle with the chili peppers and scallions (spring onions) and continue broiling for a further 5–10 minutes.

PORK CURRY
WITH FRESH HERBS

Ingredients

3 tbsp oil

1½ lb / 700 g lean pork (without skin or bones) diced

Salt & freshly milled pepper

1 onion, diced

1 dried chili, finely chopped

2 tsp finely grated fresh ginger

A good pinch of ground coriander

½ tsp ground curcuma (turmeric)

A good pinch of ground cumin

A pinch of ground cloves

¾ cup / 200 ml water

2 tbsp dark soy sauce

1 tbsp chopped parsley

Scallion (spring onion) greens, cut into rings

Method
Prep and cook time: 1 hour

1 Heat the oil and quickly brown the meat on all sides. Season with salt and pepper and add the onion, ginger and chili. Fry gently for about 3 minutes.

2 Then stir in the coriander, curcuma (turmeric), cumin and cloves, and add ¾–1 cup / 200 ml water and the soy sauce. Cover and cook for about 45 minutes.

3 Serve sprinkled with parsley and scallion (spring onion) rings.

CHICKEN WINGS IN HOISIN SAUCE

Ingredients

12 chicken wings

Salt and freshly ground pepper, to taste

1 tbsp honey

1 tbsp hoisin sauce

2 cloves garlic, minced

1 inch / 3-cm piece fresh ginger root, peeled and grated

To garnish:

1 tbsp sesame seeds

4 scallions (spring onions), chopped

1 lemon, cut into wedges

Method

Prep and cook time: 1 hour

1 Pre-heat the oven to 375°F (180°C / Gas Mark 5).

2 Place the chicken wings in an ovenproof dish. Season with salt and pepper.

3 To prepare the sauce, in a small bowl, combine the honey, hoisin sauce, garlic and ginger with 3 tbsp water. Spread over the chicken wings and toss to coat. Let marinate for 15 minutes.

4 Roast the chicken for 30 minutes, brushing occasionally with the marinade, until well browned and cooked through. Serve at once, sprinkled with the sesame seeds and chopped scallions (spring onions) and garnished with lemon wedges.

SICHUAN BEEF

Ingredients

1 lb / 450 g rump or round steak, thinly sliced

Salt and freshly ground black pepper, to taste

3 tbsp rice wine or dry sherry

2 tbsp vegetable oil

1 onion, chopped

2 cloves garlic, minced

1 inch / 3-cm piece fresh ginger root, peeled and grated

2 large carrots, cut into matchsticks

1 (8-oz) / 250 g head of broccoli, stalks peeled and cut into small florets

2 tbsp oyster sauce

Method

Prep and cook time: 25 min

1 In a medium bowl, season the steak with salt and pepper and toss together with the wine or sherry. Cover and leave to marinate for 5 minutes.

2 Heat the oil in a large wok or skillet; add onion and stir-fry until translucent, a few minutes. Add the garlic, ginger and carrots and continue cooking for 2 minutes until softened slightly.

3 Stir in the beef and its juices, the wine or sherry, and broccoli; stir-fry for 3–5 minutes, until the meat is browned and the broccoli is tender-crisp.

4 Pour over the oyster sauce and cook, stirring to coat, 1–2 minutes more, until heated through. Serve immediately.

BEAN CURRY WITH PORK

Ingredients

1 lb 2 oz / 500 g green beans

14 oz / 400 g pork (escalope)

3–4 tbsp yellow curry paste

4 oz / 100 g bacon, in slices

1 lb 2 oz / 500 g cooked potatoes

2 tbsp oil

1 tbsp onion, diced

1¾ cups / 400 ml unsweetened coconut milk

Dill weed (dill), to taste

Red chili, chopped, to taste

Salt & pepper

Method

Prep and cook time: 30 min

1 Trim the beans and cut into pieces, then blanch in boiling salted water for 3–5 minutes. Refresh in ice-cold water and drain.

2 Dice the meat and mix with the curry paste.

3 Cut the bacon into strips.

4 Peel and dice the potatoes.

5 Break the dill weed into small pieces.

6 Heat the oil in a deep skillet or wok, add the bacon and fry for 2–3 minutes. Then add the meat and onion and fry the meat on all sides, stirring constantly. Add the coconut milk and the prepared vegetables. Bring to a boil, stirring occasionally, and simmer for 5 minutes. Add some dill weed, season with salt and pepper and add chili to taste. Spoon into bowls and serve garnished with more dill weed.

NOODLES WITH VEGETABLES AND PORK

Ingredients

4 oz / 100 g thin egg noodles

2 tbsp vegetable oil

12 oz / 350 g ground pork

Soy sauce, to taste

Cayenne pepper, to taste

1–2 tbsp sesame oil

2 cloves garlic, minced

2 scallions (spring onions), thinly sliced

1 inch / 3-cm fresh ginger root, peeled and finely chopped

7 oz / 200 g shiitake mushrooms, quartered

1 cup / 150 g snow peas (mangetout), halved diagonally

1 cup / 150 g thinly sliced Chinese cabbage leaves

²/₃ cup / 150 g bamboo shoots, rinsed and drained

Method

Prep and cook time: 45 min

1 Cook the noodles in salted water according to package instructions. Rinse in a colander under running water; drain.

2 Heat the vegetable oil in a large skillet or wok; add the pork and cook, stirring constantly, until no longer pink. Season with soy sauce and cayenne, remove from the skillet and set aside to keep warm.

3 Return the skillet to the heat and add the sesame oil. Add the garlic, scallions (spring onions), ginger, mushrooms, snow peas (mangetout), cabbage and bamboo shoots and stir-fry for 2–3 minutes.

4 Add the reserved pork and noodles and continue frying for a further 2 minutes. Season to taste with additional soy sauce and cayenne and serve at once.

CHICKEN
WITH DATES AND MANGO

Ingredients

2 tbsp oil

1 tbsp garam masala

Salt

1 tbsp honey

Cayenne pepper

8 chicken legs (drumsticks)

1 cup mixed rice/200 g (basmati and brown rice)

2½ cups/about 600 ml chicken broth (stock)

2 shallots

1 mango

1/3 cup/50 g dried dates, roughly chopped

Curry powder: a good pinch of ginger, turmeric, cardamom, mace, nutmeg, cinnamon and cumin, all ground

1 tbsp parsley, chopped

1 tbsp mint, chopped

Mint leaves to garnish

Method

Prep and cook time: 45 min

1 Mix the oil with the garam masala, salt, honey and cayenne pepper and brush the chicken with the mixture. Put the chicken under a preheated broiler (grill) for about 30 minutes, turning occasionally, until cooked.

2 Meanwhile put the rice into a pan with the chicken broth (stock) and bring to a boil.

3 Peel and chop the shallots and add to the rice.

4 Peel and halve the mango and remove the pit. Dice the flesh and add to the rice after about 20 minutes. Then add the dates and continue cooking gently for 5-10 minutes more, until done. Season with the curry powder, salt and cayenne pepper. Finally stir in the chopped parsley and mint.

5 Serve the chicken drumsticks in bowls on the rice and garnish with mint.

LAMB BIRYANI

Ingredients

1½ lb / 650 g lamb (leg)

7 tbsp ghee or clarified butter

1–2 onions, finely diced

2 tsp freshly grated ginger

3 cloves garlic, pressed

6 cardamom pods

5 cloves

1 piece cinnamon stick (¾-1 inch / 2–3 cm)

½ tsp ground cumin

½ tsp curcuma (turmeric)

Chili powder, to taste

⅔ cup / 150 g yogurt

⅔ cup / 150 ml meat broth (stock)

Salt

1½ cups / 300 g basmati rice

⅓ cup / 50 g raisins

4 tbsp milk

A few saffron threads

6 tbsp blanched almonds

Cilantro (coriander) leaves to garnish

Method

Prep and cook time: 2 hours 15 min

1 Cut the meat into bite-size pieces. Heat 4 tablespoons ghee (or clarified butter) in a pan and sauté half of the onions until translucent. Add the ginger, cardamom, garlic, cloves, cinnamon and meat and fry, stirring frequently, until the meat is lightly browned on all sides. Stir in the ground spices, yogurt and broth (stock) and season with salt. Cover and simmer over a low heat for 45–60 minutes, stirring occasionally (it will be very thick).

2 Sauté the rest of the onions in a pan without letting them color. Wash the rice in a sieve under running water and add to the onions with just double the amount of lightly salted water. Bring to a boil and cook, covered, over a very low heat for about 5 minutes.

3 Put the meat into a greased baking dish. Drain the rice and mix with the raisins. Heat the milk, add the saffron and 2 tablespoons ghee and let them dissolve. Add the milk to the rice and mix with the meat in the dish.

4 Put a lid on the dish (or seal with aluminum foil) and cook in a preheated oven (350°F / 180°C / Gas Mark 4, middle shelf) for about 1 hour.

5 Lightly toast the almonds in the remaining ghee and add to the dish.

6 Before serving fluff up the lamb biryani with a fork, season to taste and spoon onto plates. Scatter some cilantro (coriander) over the top and serve.

RED BEEF CURRY

Ingredients

3 tbsp oil

1–2 tsp shrimp paste

½ tsp chili flakes

1 tsp ginger, freshly grated

1 onion, finely diced

2 cloves garlic, minced

1 lb 6 oz / 600 g beef, e. g. rump, cut into strips

1 cup / 250 ml coconut milk

14 oz / 400 g sweet potatoes, peeled and roughly chopped

2 red bell peppers, deseeded and cut into strips

1½ cups / 250 g string beans, trimmed

2 kaffir lime leaves

Salt

Light soy sauce

Method

Prep and cook time: 50 min

1 Fry the shrimp paste, chili, ginger, onion and garlic in hot oil.

2 Add the meat and fry, then pour in the coconut milk. Add a little water and the vegetables.

3 Throw in the lime leaves and simmer gently for about 30 minutes, stirring occasionally. Add a little water if needed. Season with salt and soy sauce and serve.

BEEF WITH CABBAGE AND MUSHROOMS

Ingredients

2 tbsp vegetable oil

10 oz / 300 g lean beef steak, sliced

½ Chinese cabbage, sliced

1 red bell pepper, sliced into strips

10 oz / 300 g Asian mushrooms (try straw, oyster, shiitake or enoki), sliced if large

2 tsp cornstarch (cornflour)

2 tsp dry sherry

Scant ½ cup / 100 ml beef broth (stock)

2 tsp dark soy sauce

Enoki mushrooms, to garnish

Method

Prep and cook time: 20 min

1 Heat the oil in a large wok or skillet, add the beef and stir-fry just until browned, 3 minutes. Add the cabbage and bell pepper and stir-fry for 1 minute. Add the mushrooms and cook for 2 minutes more; set aside and keep warm.

2 In a small bowl, mix the cornstarch (conflour) with the sherry to a smooth paste.

3 In a medium saucepan, combine the broth (stock) and soy sauce; stir in the cornstarch mixture. Bring to a boil and cook, stirring, until the sauce is thickened.

4 Add the sauce to the beef and vegetables; heat through and serve at once, garnished with enoki mushrooms.

SPICY PORK VINDALOO

Ingredients

1 tbsp mustard oil

1 lb 12 oz / 800 g pork (e. g. shoulder), diced

2 onions, finely diced

2 cloves garlic, finely diced

1 tsp ginger, freshly grated

1/2 tsp cumin

1/2 tsp curcuma (tumeric)

1 stick cinnamon

1 lemon, juice

1 tsp tamarind paste

1 tsp brown sugar

2/3 cup / 150 ml water

1 new potato, to garnish

oil, for frying

Method

Prep and cook time: I hour

1 Heat the mustard oil and fry the meat in it. Add the onions, garlic and the spices and sauté.

2 Pour in the lemon juice, stir in the tamarind paste and sugar and add about 2/3 cup (150 ml) water. Cover and simmer gently over a low heat for 45–50 minutes. Add a little more water if needed.

3 For the garnish, slice the potato into very thin sticks and fry in hot oil until golden brown. Drain on a paper towel and lightly salt.

4 Season the curry, garnish with the potato sticks and serve.

CHICKEN WITH OYSTER SAUCE AND NOODLES

Ingredients

400 g / 1 lb udon noodles

600 g / 1½ lb skinless boneless chicken breasts, chopped into bite-size pieces

Salt and freshly ground pepper, to taste

5 tbsp sesame oil, divided

4-inch / 10-cm piece lemongrass

1 garlic clove, minced

1 scallion (spring onion), finely chopped

3 tbsp oyster sauce

2 tbsp light soy sauce

1 tsp sugar

Method

Prep and cook time: 25 min plus 30 min to marinate

1 Cook the noodles in boiling salted water according to package instructions; drain and set aside.

2 In a small bowl, mix the chicken with salt, pepper, lemongrass and 2 tbsp of the sesame oil; marinate for 30 minutes.

3 Heat the remaining 3 tbsp oil in a wok or large skillet and stir-fry the garlic and the scallion (spring onion) for 30 seconds. Add the chicken and fry all together for 2–3 minutes, until the chicken is cooked through. Season with oyster sauce, soy sauce and sugar; discard the lemongrass stalk.

4 Toss the noodles with the chicken and the sauce and heat through; serve at once.

BEEF CURRY
WITH POTATOES
AND NUTS

Ingredients

1lb 6oz / 600 g beef

2 shallots, finely chopped

2 cloves garlic, finely chopped

3 tbsp sesame oil

2 dried red chilis

½ cup / 50 g peanuts, fresh, not salted

3 cups/800 ml coconut cream

14 oz/400 g boiling potatoes

4 tbsp fish sauce

1 tbsp oyster sauce

2 tbsp brown sugar

2 tbsp lime juice

4 slices of lime, fried

For the curry paste:

1 shallot, peeled

2 cloves garlic, peeled

I inch / 4 cm galangal

2 red chilis

1 tsp shrimp paste

Salt

Method

Prep and cook time: 1 hour 30 min

1 For the curry paste, crush the shallot and garlic with the galangal and chili in a mortar until smooth or process in a blender. Stir in the shrimp paste and salt to taste. Set aside.

2 Cut the beef into thin strips.

3 Heat 1 tablespoon of the oil in a wok and fry the shallots, the garlic and the chilis over a high heat until the shallots are golden brown. Take out of the wok. Let cool slightly, then place in the mortar and crush to a smooth paste.

4 Put the peanuts in the wok and toast until golden brown. Transfer the peanuts to a clean mortar and crush.

5 Fry the meat in the remaining oil over a high heat and pour in half of the coconut cream. Bring to a boil, then reduce the heat and simmer for 45 minutes.

6 In the meantime peel the potatoes and cut into about 1 inch (3 cm) cubes. Take the meat and the sauce out of the wok and clean the wok.

7 Sauté the curry paste in the wok, pour in the remaining coconut cream, add the potatoes, the crushed peanuts and the shallot paste and bring to a boil. Cook for 5 minutes, then add the meat and season with fish sauce, oyster sauce and sugar. Simmer for about 25 minutes over a medium heat until the potatoes are cooked.

8 Season to taste with lime juice and spoon into bowls. Garnish with fried lime slices and serve.

CHICKEN WITH ORANGE ZEST

Ingredients

2 oranges

2 cloves garlic, chopped

4 skinless boneless chicken breasts, cut into bite-size cubes

400 g / 1 lb glass (bean thread, cellophane) noodles

1 tbsp cornstarch (cornflour)

3 tbsp sesame oil

1 tbsp honey

Light soy sauce, to taste

Cayenne pepper, to taste

1 scallion (spring onion), green parts only, very thinly sliced on the diagonal, to garnish

Method

Prep and cook time: 30 min plus 12 hours to marinate

1 Finely grate the zest of one orange and remove the zest of the other in fine strips. Juice both oranges.

2 In a medium bowl, mix together the grated orange zest, orange juice and garlic. Add chicken and toss to coat. Cover and marinate in the refrigerator at least 8 hours or overnight.

3 Cook the noodles according to the instructions on the package; rinse in a colander under cold running water, drain and set aside.

4 Remove the chicken from the marinade and drain well, reserving the marinade. Spread the cornstarch (cornflour) on a plate and toss with the chicken to coat the chicken.

5 Heat the oil in a wok or skillet until smoking, then add the chicken and cook, stirring, until browned all over. Add the honey and heat through. Pour in the reserved marinade and cook, stirring to loosen browned bits from the bottom of the skillet. Simmer, stirring frequently, for about 3–4 minutes or until the chicken is cooked.

6 Season with soy sauce and cayenne pepper and add the orange zest strips.

7 Place the drained noodles on plates or a large platter. Arrange the orange chicken on top and sprinkle with the scallion rings. Serve at once.

CHICKEN TIKKA MASALA

Ingredients

1 oven-ready chicken, 2½–3 lb
/ 1.2–1.4 kg

1 lemon

Salt & freshly milled pepper

For the marinade:

2 tsp freshly grated ginger

2 cloves garlic, crushed

2 cups / 500 g yogurt

2 tbsp vegetable oil

2 tbsp paprika

Spice mixture: ½ tsp ground cumin,
black pepper, chili powder and
curcuma (turmeric)

1 tbsp cilantro (coriander) leaves,
chopped

Method

Prep and cook time: 1 hour 15 min plus
8 hours to marinate

1 Joint the chicken into 6–8 pieces. Score the surface of
the chicken pieces to a depth of ¼ inch (5 mm) and put
into a shallow dish. Sprinkle with pepper, salt and the
juice of a lemon. Let stand for about 30 minutes.

2 Mix all the spices for the marinade with the yogurt
and oil. Coat the chicken pieces generously with
the marinade and seal the dish with aluminum foil.
Marinate the chicken in the refrigerator for 8 hours
or overnight.

3 Preheat the oven to 350°F (180°C / Gas Mark 4).
Line a cookie sheet with aluminum foil and put the
chicken pieces on the sheet. Reserve the marinade.
Cook the chicken in the oven for 35–40 minutes,
brushing frequently with marinade (using about a
quarter), and adding a little water if necessary.

4 Heat the remaining marinade in a large pan and add
the chicken pieces. Continue to heat very gently for
5 minutes, then sprinkle with cilantro (coriander) and
serve with rice.

DUCK BREAST WITH CELERY

Ingredients

1 tbsp hoisin sauce

2 tbsp rice wine or dry sherry

1 tsp orange juice

½ tsp cornstarch (cornflour)

450 g / 1 lb skinless boneless duck breasts, sliced into matchsticks

2 tbsp vegetable oil

2 cloves garlic, minced

5 stalks celery, cut into matchsticks

2 scallions (spring onions), thinly sliced

1 red bell pepper, sliced into thin strips

Method

Prep and cook time: 15 min plus 1 hour to marinate

1 In a medium bowl, mix the hoisin sauce, rice wine or sherry, the orange juice and cornstarch (cornflour). Add the duck and toss to coat well. Cover and chill for 1 hour.

2 Heat the oil in a wok or large skillet and stir-fry the garlic for 1 minute.

3 Add the duck and stir-fry, keeping the heat high, until cooked through, about 5 minutes.

4 Add the celery, scallions (spring onions) and bell pepper and stir-fry for 2 more minutes, until the vegetables are softened. Serve at once.

TANDOORI CHICKEN KEBABS
WITH RAITA

Ingredients

4 chicken breast fillets

1 lemon

Salt & freshly milled pepper

For the marinade:

2 cloves garlic

Scant 1 cup / 200 g yogurt

2 tbsp vegetable oil

2 tsp freshly grated ginger

2 tsp paprika

Spice mixture: 1 tsp each of ground: cumin, nutmeg, cilantro (coriander), black pepper, paprika

For the raita:

1 cucumber

1 cup / 250 g yogurt

½ tsp ground caraway

½ tsp ground coriander

1 tbsp finely chopped parsley

1 tbsp finely chopped mint

Salt & freshly milled pepper

Mint, to garnish

Method

Prep and cook time: 30 min plus 8 hours to marinate

1 Cut the chicken into bite-size cubes and put into a shallow dish. Sprinkle with pepper, salt and lemon juice and let stand for about 30 minutes.

2 Peel the garlic. Mix the yogurt with the oil and the spices to make a marinade and press the garlic into it. Coat the chicken generously with the marinade and seal the dish with aluminum foil. Marinate in the refrigerator for 8 hours or overnight.

3 For the raita, peel the cucumber, halve lengthways, scrape out the seeds and grate the cucumber. Mix with the yogurt, add the caraway, coriander, parsley and mint and season with salt and pepper. Let stand for about 1 hour. Garnish with mint.

4 Thread the chicken onto skewers. Preheat a broiler (grill). Lay aluminum foil on the grill rack and put the kebabs on the foil. Grill for 8–10 minutes, or until the chicken is cooked through, brushing with marinade from time to time.

5 Serve the chicken kebabs with the raita.

MUGHLAI LAMB KORMA

Ingredients

1 cup / 250 ml full-fat yogurt

1 tsp salt

2 tsp ground cumin

1 tsp ground coriander

A pinch of cayenne pepper

Freshly milled pepper

4 tbsp freshly chopped cilantro (coriander)

5 tbsp olive oil

1 bay leaf

6 cardamom pods

Cinnamon stick (2 inches / about 5 cm)

2 lb / 900 g lamb, from the shoulder, without bones, cut into bite-size cubes

1 onion, chopped

4 tbsp golden raisins

2 tbsp sour cream

A pinch of ground cardamom

Method

Prep and cook time: 1 hour 30 min

1 Mix the yogurt with the salt, cumin, ground coriander, cayenne pepper, black pepper and fresh cilantro (coriander) leaves and set aside.

2 Heat the oil in a large skillet. When the oil is hot add the bay leaf, cardamom pods, cinnamon and diced meat. Brown the meat on all sides over a medium heat. If the skillet is not big enough to take all the meat at once, fry the meat a few pieces at a time so that it has plenty of room in the skillet.

3 Take the meat out of the skillet and keep warm. Sauté the onion until translucent in the oil left in the skillet.

4 Return the meat to the skillet with the spices, add the yogurt mixture and golden raisins and bring to a boil. Cover and cook over a low heat for 60–70 minutes, until the meat is very tender. Then remove the lid and cook over a high heat until the sauce is reduced to the desired consistency.

5 Stir in the sour cream, season with the ground cardamom and serve at once.

PAD THAI WITH BEEF

Ingredients

8 oz / 225 g dried rice noodles

2 tbsp oil

3 cloves garlic, chopped

2 tsp chopped red chilies

14 oz / 400 g beef, for pan-frying, cut into thin strips

2 tbsp fish sauce

2 tbsp lime juice

2 tsp brown sugar

$1/3$ cup / 40 g soybean sprouts

¼ cup / 40 g frozen peas

¼ cup / 40 g canned soybeans, drained

Green scallion (spring onion) stalks, to garnish

Method

Prep and cook time: 30 min

1 Soak the noodles in warm water for 10 minutes, then drain and set aside.

2 Heat the oil in a wok or a large skillet. Add the garlic, chilies and beef and stir-fry for about 4 minutes. Add the drained noodles, cover and fry for a further minute.

3 Add the fish sauce, lime juice and sugar and stir well until everything is heated evenly. Add the soybean sprouts, peas and soybeans and cook until done.

4 Check the seasoning and serve garnished with the green stalks of scallion (spring onion) cut into rings at an angle.

LAMB WITH YOGURT SAUCE

Ingredients

2 lb 4 oz / 1 kg lamb, e.g. shoulder

3 tbsp ghee or clarified butter

2 onions, diced

2 cloves garlic, finely chopped

1 tsp curcuma (turmeric)

1 tbsp paprika, noble sweet

Spice mixture: 1 good pinch each of ground: cumin, coriander seeds, allspice, cloves and cinnamon

1 cup / 250 g yogurt

For the rice:

1¼ cups / 250 g basmati rice

4 cardamom pods

4 cloves

1 cinnamon stick

2 fresh bay leaves

1 tsp curcuma (turmeric)

For the yogurt sauce:

1¾ cups / 400 g yogurt

Juice of 1 lemon

1 tbsp mint leaves, chopped

Salt

Method
Prep and cook time: 2 hours

1 Cut the lamb into large cubes.

2 Heat the ghee (or clarified butter) and brown the meat over a fairly high heat. Add the onions, garlic and spices. Deglaze with a little water and add the yogurt. Cover and cook in the oven at 350°F (180°C / Gas Mark 4) for about 1½ hours. Stir occasionally and add more water if necessary.

3 Meanwhile, put the rice into a pan with the spices. Add double the amount of water, cover and bring to a boil. Simmer for about 25 minutes, until cooked.

4 For the yogurt sauce, mix all the ingredients and season to taste with salt.

5 Take the lid off the curry and let brown for about 10 minutes. Check the seasoning and serve with the rice, the yogurt sauce and poppadoms.

CHICKEN WITH CHILIES AND BASIL

Ingredients

4 chicken breasts

2 shallots

2 chilies

1 tbsp sesame oil

Light soy sauce

Fish sauce

½ bunch Thai basil, for garnish

Method

Prep and cook time: 30 min

1 Cut the chicken into bite-size pieces.

2 Halve and deseed the chilies and cut into very thin strips. Peel and halve the shallots and slice lengthwise.

3 Heat the oil and brown the meat on all sides. Add the shallots and sauté until translucent.

4 Add the chilies and soy sauce and fish sauce to taste, then cook over a very low heat until the meat is done. Finally mix in the basil leaves and serve in bowls.

CHICKEN SATAY AND GINGER-COCONUT SAUCE

Ingredients

8 chicken legs

3 tbsp oil

1 tsp spice mixture, (equal parts of ground ginger, black and white pepper, cayenne pepper)

3 shallots, finely diced

2 cloves garlic, finely chopped

1 tsp ginger, freshly grated

2 chilies, finely chopped

$2/3$ cup / 150 ml white wine

1 cup / 240 ml coconut milk

1 tbsp honey

8 oz / 225 g tub of crème fraîche

Salt & freshly milled pepper

1 tbsp fish sauce

2 tbsp cilantro (coriander), chopped

Kebab skewers

Method

Prep and cook time: 40 min

1 Skin, wash and dry the chicken legs, take the meat off the bone and dice.

2 Mix 2 tablespoons of oil with the spice mixture and mix with the chicken. Cover and chill.

3 Heat the rest of the oil and sauté the shallots and garlic without browning. Stir in the ginger and chili, then add the white wine.

4 Boil until reduced, then add the coconut milk, honey and crème fraîche and simmer, stirring occasionally, to produce a creamy sauce. Strain through a sieve, add the cilantro (coriander) and add seasoning and fish sauce to taste.

5 Thread the chicken onto skewers and fry or grill for about 5–6 minutes, turning frequently, until cooked. Put on plates and pour the sauce over.

LAMB SHANK
WITH PRUNES AND APRICOTS

Ingredients

4 lamb shanks

1 stalk celery

1 leek

2 carrots

2 onions

2 cloves garlic

2 oz/50 g ghee or clarified butter

2 bay leaves

2 sprigs fresh thyme

2 sprigs fresh rosemary

14 fl oz /400 ml dry white wine

14 fl oz/400 ml lamb broth (stock)

3–4 oz/100 g prunes, pitted

3–4 oz/100 g dried apricots, pitted

7 fl oz/200 g light (single) cream

1–2 tbsp. yellow mild curry powder

1–2 tbsp. cornstarch (cornflour)

Salt & freshly milled pepper

Method

Prep and cook time: 3 hours 30 min

1 Pre-heat the oven to 300°F/150°C/gas mark 2. Cut some of the fat off the lamb shanks, then season with salt and pepper. Wash and trim the celery and leek and roughly chop. Peel and roughly chop the carrots, onions and garlic.

2 Heat the ghee or clarified butter in a roasting pan and fry the lamb shanks on all sides until browned. Remove the meat, then fry the prepared vegetables and add the bay leaves and the herbs. Fry over a high heat until browned, stirring continually. Pour in the wine and reduce until the liquid has almost evaporated. Now pour in the lamb broth (stock) and place the lamb shanks in the roasting pan again. Cover and roast in the pre-heated oven for about 2½ hours. Add a little water or broth if necessary.

3 In the meantime soak the prunes and apricots in lukewarm water.

4 Remove the meat from the roasting pan, cover and keep warm.

5 Strain the pan juices through a fine-mesh sieve. Spoon off some of the fat, then add the apricots and the prunes and bring to a boil. Pour in the cream, stir in the curry powder and simmer for about 10 minutes. Mix the cornstarch (cornflour) with a few drops of cold water until smooth then stir into the sauce to thicken. Season with salt and pepper and serve with the lamb shanks.

PORK WITH PLUM SAUCE

Ingredients

1 lb 12 oz / 800 g pork loin,
cut into strips

2 tsp sesame oil

2 carrots, peeled and sliced into
thin strips

1 clove garlic, minced

1 inch / 3-cm piece fresh ginger root,
peeled and grated

2 tbsp soy sauce, plus more to taste

2–3 tbsp plum sauce

Garnish:

1 scallion (spring onion), thinly sliced
on the diagonal

Chopped fresh parsley

Method

Prep and cook time: 25 min

1 Heat the oil in a wok or large skillet until very hot. Add the pork and cook, turning occasionally, until browned on all sides.

2 Add the carrots, garlic, ginger, soy sauce and a little water; heat through.

3 Stir in the plum sauce and simmer for 3–4 minutes, stirring occasionally.

4 Season the meat with soy sauce and serve garnished with scallion (spring onion) and parsley.

FRIED PORK
WITH VEGETABLES AND HOISIN SAUCE

Ingredients

1 tbsp sesame oil

1 inch / 3 cm piece fresh
ginger root, grated

1 clove garlic, minced

1 red onion, sliced

1 lb / 450 g lean pork,
cut into strips

1 red bell pepper,
coarsely chopped

1 yellow bell pepper,
coarsely chopped

4 oz / 100 g chestnut or brown
button mushrooms, quartered

2 tbsp sweet chili sauce

2 tbsp dark soy sauce

2 tbsp teriyaki sauce

7 oz / 200 g snow peas
(mangetout)

For the fried rice:

1 egg

2 tsp sesame oil

2 tbsp vegetable oil

1 cup / 200 g cooked long-
grain rice

Salt and freshly ground pepper,
to taste

½ cup / 400 g thawed
frozen peas

4 scallions (spring onions),
finely chopped

2 tsp light soy sauce

Method
Prep and cook time: 30 min

1 Heat the sesame oil in a large wok or skillet;
add the ginger, garlic and onion, stir-fry for
2 minutes.

2 Add the pork and fry for 5 minutes, turning as
needed, until browned. Add the red and yellow
peppers and the mushrooms into the wok and
cook, stirring, for another 5 minutes.

3 Pour in the sweet chili sauce, soy sauce
and teriyaki sauce, then add the snow peas
(mangetout). Cook for a further 2–3 minutes; set
aside and keep warm.

4 For the fried rice, beat together the egg and
sesame oil in a small bowl and set aside.

5 Heat the vegetable oil in a clean wok or
skillet, then add the rice and stir-fry for about
3–4 minutes.

6 Add the peas and scallions (spring onions)
and stir-fry for about 3 minutes. Season with salt
and pepper and splash in the soy sauce, then
push to one side of the wok.

7 Pour the beaten egg mixture into the other
side of the wok and leave for about 10 seconds
so it begins to set. Using a chopstick, briskly
swirl around the egg to break it up, then toss it
gently with the rice. Stir-fry for a further minute
and serve at once with the pork and vegetables.

RED CHICKEN CURRY

Ingredients

For the red curry paste:

About 1 inch / 2.5 cm galangal

1 shallot, peeled

1 clove garlic, peeled

About 1 inch / 2.5 cm lemongrass

2 Thai chilis

Zest of a kaffir lime

½–1 tsp shrimp paste

Salt

1 lb 6 oz / 600 g chicken breasts

3 tomatoes

1 cup / 200 g pineapple pieces

2 stalks lemongrass

1 tbsp oil

1¾ cups / 400 ml unsweetened coconut milk

1 tbsp brown sugar

3 tbsp fish sauce

2 tbsp lime juice

Method

Prep and cook time: 30 min

1 For the red curry paste place all the ingredients except for the shrimp paste and the salt in a mortar and finely crush. Now mix in the salt and the shrimp paste and stir until smooth.

2 Cut the chicken breasts into 1 inch (2.5 cm) pieces. Place the tomatoes into boiling water, then immediately into cold water. Peel, quarter, de-seed and chop the tomatoes. Chop the pineapple into small pieces. Trim the lemongrass, then finely chop.

3 Heat the oil in a wok or skillet. Fry the curry paste, then pour in the coconut milk and bring to a boil. Season with lemongrass, sugar, fish sauce and lime juice. Add the chicken pieces and the pineapple and simmer for about 5 minutes. Now add the tomatoes and heat until the chicken is cooked.

4 Divide into 4 bowls and serve.

ROAST PORK
WITH VEGETABLES

Ingredients

For the marinade:

4 tbsp light soy sauce

2 tbsp rice wine or dry sherry

2 tbsp hoisin sauce

2 cloves garlic, minced

1 inch / 3 cm piece fresh ginger root, peeled and grated

3 tbsp honey, divided

1 lb / 450 g pork loin

For the stir-fry:

2 tbsp sesame oil, divided

4 scallions (spring onions), thinly sliced

4 carrots, sliced into thin sticks

1 red bell pepper, cut into thin strips

7 oz / 200 g snow peas or sugar snap peas, sliced into thin strips

Method

Prep and cook time: 45 min plus 2 hours marinating

1 To prepare the marinade, mix together the soy sauce, rice wine or dry sherry, hoisin sauce, garlic, ginger and 1 tbsp of the honey in a medium bowl. Add the pork to the bowl and turn to coat well. Cover and marinate in the refrigerator for 2 hours.

2 Pre-heat the oven to 375°F (190°C / Gas Mark 5). Half fill a roasting pan with water and rest a rack on top.

3 In a small bowl, combine the remaining 2 tbsp of honey with 1 tbsp sesame oil and 3 tbsp of the marinade.

4 Put the pork onto the rack and brush with the honey-marinade mixture. Roast for 15 minutes, brush over more of the honey marinade and roast for 20 more minutes until the pork is cooked.

5 Meanwhile, heat the remaining 1 tbsp sesame oil in a large skillet or wok. Add the scallions, carrots, bell pepper and snow peas or sugar snaps and cook for 5 minutes until the vegetables are slightly softened but still crunchy.

6 Bring the remaining marinade to a boil and cook, stirring, until slightly reduced, 5 minutes.

7 Slice the pork and serve on a bed of vegetables with a little of the cooked marinade poured over.

KUNG PAO SPICY CHICKEN WITH PEANUTS

Ingredients

3 tbsp vegetable oil

4 skinless boneless chicken breasts, cut into cubes

3 red chili peppers, seeded and sliced into thin strips

3 garlic cloves, roughly chopped

2 scallions (spring onions), finely chopped

½ cup / 75 g peanuts

1 tsp sugar

2 tbsp rice wine

Soy sauce, to taste

Method

Prep and cook time: 20 min

1 In a large skillet or wok, heat the vegetable oil until very hot. Add the chicken and chilies and stir-fry until the chicken is seared, 2–3 minutes.

2 Add the garlic, scallions (spring onions), peanuts and sugar and continue frying for 1–2 minutes.

3 Add the rice wine and a little water, if needed, and simmer for 1–2 minutes, until cooked. Season with soy sauce and serve at once.

PORK CURRY WITH TAMARIND

Ingredients

For the curry paste:

2 green chilies

1 tsp shrimp paste

1 tsp ground curcuma (turmeric)

1 tsp freshly grated ginger

For the curry:

2 oz / 50 g pressed tamarinds

2 onions

1 lb 6 oz / 600 g pork

2 tbsp fish sauce

2 tbsp oil

14 oz / 400 ml can unsweetened coconut milk

Salt

Sugar

½ bunch Thai basil, to garnish

Method

Prep and cook time: 55 min plus 30 min soaking time

1 Put all the curry paste ingredients into a mortar and grind to a paste.

2 Soak the tamarinds in ½ cup (120 ml) water for about 30 minutes. Peel and finely slice the onions. Cut the meat into bite-size cubes. Put into a bowl with the fish sauce and let stand for 10 minutes.

3 Heat the oil in a large skillet and brown the meat on all sides in batches. Take the creamy top of the coconut milk and put into a pan. Add the rest of the coconut milk to the skillet with the meat, cover and simmer for about 20 minutes.

4 Bring the coconut cream to a boil in the pan and simmer for 2 minutes. Add 2 tablespoons of the curry paste and stir until dissolved. Add the onions and cook for about 1 minute. Transfer the meat and coconut sauce from the skillet to the pan.

5 Squeeze out the tamarind, discard the fibers and add the liquid to the curry. Simmer for about 15 minutes, until the meat is cooked. Add salt and sugar to taste.

6 Garnish with Thai basil and serve.

DUCK WITH BOK CHOY

Ingredients

4 tbsp sesame oil, divided

1 clove garlic, minced

1 chili pepper, seeded and chopped

1 inch / 3-cm piece fresh ginger root, minced

2 boneless duck breasts, each around 12 oz / 350 g

Salt and freshly ground pepper

1 red bell pepper, seeded and roughly chopped

1 yellow bell pepper, seeded and roughly chopped

4 scallions (spring onions), sliced into rings

1 lb 8 oz / 600 g bok choy, white parts chopped and green parts thinly sliced

2 tbsp soy sauce, plus more to taste

1 tbsp sesame paste

1 tsp honey

1 tsp rice vinegar

Method

Prep and cook time: 1 hour plus 1 hour to marinate

1 In a medium bowl, combine 2 tbsp of the sesame oil with the garlic, chili pepper and ginger to make a marinade. Add the duck breasts and toss to coat. Cover and marinate in the refrigerator 1 hour.

2 Preheat the oven to 250°F (120°C / Gas Mark 1).

3 Place the duck breasts skin side down in a skillet and fry over medium heat for 6 to 8 minutes until golden brown. Turn over and cook for a further minute, then season with salt and pepper.

4 Place the duck breasts on a wire rack in a roasting pan in the oven and roast for 20–25 minutes.

5 Meanwhile, return the skillet to the heat and add the remaining 2 tbsp sesame oil. Add the red and yellow bell peppers and scallions (spring onions) and stir-fry until softened. Add the bok choy and continue frying for 2–3 minutes.

6 Add 2 tbsp soy sauce, the sesame paste, honey and rice vinegar and bring to a boil. Season to taste with soy sauce, salt and pepper.

7 Remove the duck from the oven, and chop into bite-size pieces. Toss with the vegetables and serve at once.

MAIN DISHES: FISH AND SEAFOOD

MUSSELS
WITH CURRY SAUCE

Ingredients

6 lb 12 oz / 3 kg mussels

2 red chilis, deseeded and cut into thin rings

2 tbsp oil

2 onions, cut into rings

4 cloves garlic, roughly chopped

A good pinch of ground cloves

½ tsp ground ginger

A good pinch of cardamom

A good pinch of caraway

½ tsp curcuma (turmeric), more if necessary

A pinch of mace

A pinch of nutmeg

A good pinch of paprika

2 pinches of cinnamon

1 cup / 250 ml pineapple juice

Scant 1½ cups / 330 ml unsweetened coconut milk

4 cups / 1 liter vegetable broth (stock)

2 tbsp chopped fresh cilantro (coriander)

2 tbsp lemon juice

Method

Prep and cook time: 45 min

1 Wash the mussels thoroughly and remove the beards. Wash again; discard any opened mussels, as they are spoilt. Drain in a colander.

2 Heat the oil in a large pan and sauté the onions, garlic and chili until the onions and garlic are transparent. Add the spices and fry briefly, then take out of the pan, leaving 1 teaspoon of the spices in the pan. Add the pineapple juice, coconut milk and ²/₃–1 cup (150–250 ml) of water and cook without a lid over a medium heat for about 10 minutes. Taste from time to time and add more water and spices if necessary to produce a creamy sauce.

3 Meanwhile, heat the broth (stock) in a large pan, add the mussels, cover and cook over a medium heat for 6–8 minutes, until the mussels have opened. Shake the pan vigorously from time to time. Discard any mussels that do not open.

4 Lift the mussels out of their cooking liquor. Stir the cilantro (coriander) into the curry sauce and add lemon juice to taste. Combine the mussels with the sauce and serve.

TANDOORI FISH MASALA

Ingredients

4 fish fillets, e.g. sea bream, cod, each weighing 7 oz / 200 g

Salt

2 tbsp lemon juice

2 tbsp ghee or clarified butter, melted

For the marinade:

2 cups / 400 g yogurt

3 tbsp vinegar

1 large onion, finely chopped

3–5 garlic cloves, crushed, according to taste

½ tsp freshly grated ginger

½–1 tsp curcuma (turmeric)

1 pinch salt

1 pinch ground coriander

1 pinch garam masala

1 pinch chili powder

Pepper, according to taste

For the garnish:

½ red chili, deseeded and cut into rings

1 tbsp scallion (spring onion) rings

1 tbsp lime zest

Method

Prep and cook time: 40 min plus 2 hours to marinate

1 Rub the fish fillets with salt and drizzle lemon juice over the top. Place the fish in a baking dish, greased with ghee or clarified butter.

2 For the marinade, mix all the ingredients together with 1–2 tablespoons water. Pour over the fish and place in the refrigerator for 2 hours. Turn the fish from time to time.

3 Pre-heat the oven to 350°F (180°C / Gas Mark 4). Put the fish in the oven and cook for about 15–20 minutes. Add a little water if needed. Before serving, place the fish under a pre-heated broiler (grill) for a few minutes to brown (according to taste).

4 Divide between 4 bowls, placing a fish fillet in the center of each bowl. Scatter a few chili and scallion (spring onion) rings over the fish and sprinkle some lime zest on the top. Serve hot.

NOODLES WITH SHRIMP AND VEGETABLES

Ingredients

1 lb / 450 g Chinese egg noodles

2 tbsp vegetable oil

5 oz / 150 g large shrimp (prawns), peeled, deveined and chopped into bite-size pieces

2 tbsp freshly chopped cilantro (fresh coriander)

1 clove garlic, minced

8 oz / 200 g bok choy, thinly sliced

1 red chili pepper, seeded and sliced into thin strips (wear gloves to prevent irritation)

1 tsp five-spice powder

2 tbsp rice wine or dry sherry

2 tbsp black bean sauce

Soy sauce, to taste

Fish sauce, to taste

Method

Prep and cook time: 30 min

1 Cook the noodles according to package instructions. Rinse in a colander under cold running water; drain and set aside.

2 Heat the oil in a large skillet or wok; add the shrimp and cilantro (coriander) and quickly stir-fry until the shrimp are barely translucent. With a slotted spoon, remove the shrimp from the wok and keep warm.

3 Return the wok to the heat and add the garlic, bok choy, chili, and five-spice powder; stir to heat through. Add the wine or sherry and about 4 tablespoons of water; bring to a boil, scraping up browned bits from the bottom of the pan.

4 Add the bean sauce and simmer for around 1–2 minutes, stirring constantly. Stir in the shrimp and noodles and cook, tossing gently to coat, until heated through. Add the soy sauce and fish sauce and season with salt and pepper.

5 Rest briefly to allow the flavors to mingle, then serve in bowls.

CLAM AND MANGOSTEEN CURRY

Ingredients

2 lbs 4 oz / 1kg fresh clams, or mixed shellfish

6 tbsp oil

3–4 cloves garlic, finely chopped

2 chilies, deseeded and chopped in half

1 cup / 240 ml water

½ cup / 120 ml fish broth (stock)

5 tbsp finely chopped Thai basil

Salt & freshly ground pepper

1–2 mangosteens

1–2 tbsp lime juice

¼ bunch chives, for garnish

6–8 kaffir lime leaves, for garnish

Method

Prep and cook time: 40 min

1 Soak the clams in a bowl of cold water for 20 minutes, to remove any sand. Scrub the clams and throw away any that have opened slightly at this stage.

2 Heat 4 tablespoons oil and sweat the garlic and one of the chilies without browning. Add the clams and heat for three minutes, until all the shells have opened. Throw away any that do not open at this stage.

3 Add the water and fish broth (stock) and cook over a low heat for 4 minutes. Remove the clams to a bowl and strain the liquid through a fine sieve to remove any last traces of sand, then return the liquid and the clams to the pan. Add the basil and the rest of the olive oil and season well with pepper and a little salt.

4 Chop the mangosteen flesh into pieces and purée finely. Put into a pan, add a little of the clam cooking liquid and heat. Add the lime juice to taste.

5 Spoon the mangosteen puree into bowls, add the clams and serve garnished with slices of the remaining chili, chives and lime leaves.

FRIED FISH
WITH GINGER, CARROTS AND SNOW PEAS

Ingredients

1 lb / 450 g firm white fish fillet such as cod or halibut, cut into strips

Salt and freshly ground pepper, to taste

2 tbsp cornstarch (cornflour)

²/₃ cup / 150 ml vegetable oil

1 inch / 3-cm piece fresh ginger root, peeled and grated

2 tbsp sesame oil

3 carrots, thinly sliced on the diagonal

7 oz / 200 g snow peas (mangetout)

4 scallions (spring onions), thinly sliced

2 tbsp rice wine or dry sherry

2 tsp sugar

Method
Prep and cook time: 25 min

1 Season the fish with salt and pepper and toss with the cornstarch (cornflour) to coat.

2 Heat the vegetable oil in a wok or large skillet until very hot. Add the fish and ginger and cook, stirring, until the fish is nearly translucent, about 3 minutes. Using a slotted spoon, remove the fish and ginger and drain on paper towels; keep warm.

3 In another skillet or wok, heat the sesame oil; add the carrots and stir-fry for 2 minutes. Add the snow peas (mangetout) and scallions (spring onions); cook for 1 more minute.

4 Add 2 tbsp water, the rice wine or sherry and the sugar and cook, stirring gently, until heated through. Add the fish to the skillet and cook gently for 1 minute, taking care not to break up the slices. Serve at once in shallow bowls.

FISH CURRY
WITH SHRIMP

Ingredients

1 tsp curcuma (turmeric)

2 tsp curry powder

1 lb / 450 g haddock, cut into bite-size pieces, skin and bones removed

4 tbsp ghee or clarified butter

2 onions, finely diced

4 garlic cloves, finely chopped

2 tsp freshly grated ginger

1 tsp mustard seeds

5 oz / 150 g canned tomatoes

½ tsp finely chopped red chili

1¾ cups / 400 ml unsweetened coconut milk

6 oz / 175 g large shrimp or prawns, peeled and ready to cook

Vegetable broth (stock)

1 tbsp finely chopped cilantro (coriander)

Method
Prep and cook time: 35 min

1 Mix the curcuma (turmeric) and curry powder and rub the fish with about half of the mixture. Reserve the remainder.

2 Heat the ghee or clarified butter in a large skillet and sauté the onions and garlic until translucent. Then add the ginger, the remaining spice mix and mustard seeds and fry briefly. Then add the tomatoes and coconut milk and simmer for about 10 minutes. Purée the sauce, but not too finely.

3 Add the chopped chili, fish and shrimp (or prawns) and cook gently for about 5 minutes, until done. If the sauce is too thick, add a little vegetable broth (stock).

4 Check the seasoning and serve garnished with cilantro (coriander).

SPICY KING PRAWNS

Ingredients

1 tbsp vegetable oil

1 inch / 3-cm piece fresh ginger, peeled and grated

2 garlic cloves, minced

2 scallions (spring onions) and chopped

1 lb / 450 g raw large shrimp (prawns), peeled and deveined

1 tbsp tomato paste

2 tsp chili bean sauce

1 tsp cider vinegar

1 tsp sugar

2 tsp sesame oil

Cilantro (fresh coriander) leaves, to garnish

Method
Prep and cook time: 20 min

1 Heat the oil in a large skillet or wok. Add the ginger, garlic and scallions (spring onions) and stir-fry for 20 seconds.

2 Add the shrimp (prawns) and stir-fry for 1 minute.

3 Add the tomato paste, chili bean sauce, cider vinegar, sugar and sesame oil and stir-fry for another few minutes. Serve at once, garnished with cilantro (coriander).

STEAMED SALMON
WITH GARLIC OIL

Ingredients

4 salmon filets with skin, each around 200 g / 7 oz

Salt and freshly ground pepper, to taste

Juice of 1 lime

4 tbsp light sesame oil

8 cloves garlic, minced

2 scallions (spring onions), chopped into 2 inch / 5-cm strips

Method

Prep and cook time: 20 min

1 Season the salmon with salt and pepper and drizzle with lime juice.

2 In a large skillet or wok, heat the oil, then add the garlic and stir-fry. As soon as the garlic begins to color, remove from the heat and stir in the scallions (spring onions). Set aside.

3 Bring 2 inches / 5 cm of water to a boil in a steamer. Place the salmon in the steamer insert, cover and steam until barely firm in the center, around 7 minutes.

4 To serve, arrange the salmon on plates, and top with the garlic-scallion mixture.

MONKFISH
AND GREEN COCONUT CURRY SAUCE

Ingredients

For the curry paste:

1 shallot, peeled

1 clove garlic, peeled

1 green chili

1 tbsp cilantro (coriander) leaves

1 tsp cilantro root, chopped

1 pinch galangal, ground

4 peppercorns

½ tsp coriander seeds

2¼ lb / 1 kg monk fish fillets

Salt

4 tbsp lemon juice

2 tbsp light soy sauce

Scant 1 cup / 200 ml unsweetened coconut milk

3–4 tbsp oil

4–5 scallions (spring onions), white part only, cut into rings

1 zucchini (courgette), thinly sliced

4 kaffir lime leaves, finely chopped

3 sprigs Thai basil

Method

Prep and cook time: 30 min plus 30 mins to marinate

1 For the curry paste, place all ingredients in a mortar and grind to a smooth paste.

2 Skin the fish and cut into 1 inch (2.5 cm) pieces. Marinate the fish pieces with the salt, lemon juice and soy sauce for about 30 minutes.

3 Heat the coconut milk over a low heat and simmer for 5 minutes. Heat the oil in a wok and fry the fish for about 4 minutes. Pour in the coconut milk and the curry paste and the rest of the marinade. (If you don't use all the curry paste, put the remainder in a jar and keep it in the refrigerator.) Reduce the heat and simmer the fish for 3 minutes.

4 Add the scallions, zucchini (courgette), some basil leaves and the lime leaves and cook for a further 3 minutes.

5 Scoop the curry onto warmed plates and garnish with the remaining basil leaves. Serve with basmati rice.

SHRIMP AND PUMPKIN CURRY

Ingredients

For the green curry paste:

1 shallot, roughly chopped

1 peeled garlic clove

1 tbsp cilantro (coriander) leaves

½ tsp coriander seeds

1 tsp freshly grated ginger

1 green chili, deseeded and roughly chopped

2 tbsp oil

1 bunch scallions (spring onions), cut into rings

2 cloves garlic, roughly chopped

2 tsp freshly chopped ginger

1 lb 6 oz / 600 g pumpkin, deseeded and chopped into ½ inch (1 cm) cubes

1¾ cups / 400 ml unsweetened coconut milk

Juice of ½ lemon

Salt & pepper

11 oz / 300 g frozen shrimp (prawns)

Method

Prep and cook time: 30 min

1 Put all the ingredients for the curry paste into a mortar and crush to make a paste.

2 Heat the oil and sauté the scallions, ginger, garlic and pumpkin over a high heat for 4–5 minutes. Stir in the coconut milk, curry paste and lemon juice, season with salt and pepper and simmer without a lid over a medium heat for about 5 minutes, until the pumpkin has softened

3 Check the seasoning, add the shrimp (prawns) and briefly return to a boil. When the shrimp are cooked, serve in bowls.

BRAISED SICHUAN FISH

Ingredients

1 tbsp sunflower or vegetable oil

1 garlic clove, chopped

7 tbsp / 100 ml fish broth (stock)

2 tbsp fish sauce

2 tbsp soy sauce

1 tsp cornstarch (cornflour), mixed to a smooth paste in 1 tbsp water

1 cup / 100 g bean sprouts, fresh or preserved, rinsed and drained

2 lb / 900 g firm white fish fillets, such as cod, plaice or halibut, chopped into 1-inch / 3-cm strips

6 scallions (spring onions), roughly chopped (reserve a few pieces for garnish)

Salt, to taste

Cayenne pepper, to taste

Method

Prep and cook time: 25 min

1 Heat the oil in a large skillet or wok; add the garlic and cook, stirring, until softened. Add the fish broth (stock), fish sauce and soy sauce and heat through.

2 Stir in the cornstarch (cornflour) mixture. Bring to a boil and cook, stirring, until slightly thickened.

3 Add the bean sprouts, fish and half of the scallions (spring onions), cover and simmer for 4–5 minutes.

4 Season with salt and cayenne pepper and serve scattered with the remaining scallions.

CHINESE-STYLE COD

Ingredients

1½ cups / 250 g baby corn

8 scallions (spring onions), cut diagonally into 2 inch / 4-cm lengths

1 red bell pepper, cut into strips

2 carrots, thinly sliced on the diagonal

2 stalks celery, sliced

2 tbsp vegetable oil

2 garlic cloves, thinly sliced

8 cod fillets (about 1 lb 12 oz / 800 g total)

2 tbsp rice wine

2 tbsp soy sauce

2 tbsp fish sauce

Salt and freshly ground pepper, to taste

Method

Prep and cook time: 45 min

1 Bring a large pot of salted water to a boil; have a bowl of ice water nearby. Working in batches, blanch the baby corn, scallions (spring onions), bell pepper, carrots and celery for around 4 minutes until al dente, remove them with a slotted spoon and refresh in cold water; drain.

2 Heat the oil in a skillet or wok, briefly fry the garlic just until fragrant, 30 seconds; remove the garlic with a slotted spoon to a plate, and return the skillet to the heat.

3 Add the fish fillets to the skillet and fry until golden brown on one side. Turn the fish over and add 4 tbsp of water, the rice wine, soy sauce and fish sauce.

4 Return the garlic to the skillet, reduce the heat and simmer for a further 1–2 minutes until the fish is cooked. Season with salt and pepper.

5 Drain the vegetables and arrange on plates. Top with the fish fillets and sauce.

SHRIMP IN BATTER
WITH CASHEWS AND RICE

Ingredients

1¼ cups / 250 g long-grain rice

½ cup / 75 g cashews

1 cup / 100 g all-purpose flour

2 eggs, separated

½ cup / 125 ml dry white wine

Vegetable oil for deep frying

1 lb 6 oz / 600 g large shrimp (prawns), peeled and deveined

Salt & freshly ground pepper

Method

Prep and cook time: 1 hour 10 min

1 Cook the rice according to package instructions; keep warm.

2 Toast the cashew nuts in a dry skillet until golden brown.

3 In a medium bowl, whisk together the flour, egg yolks and wine to make a smooth batter and season with salt and pepper. Let rest for 30 minutes.

4 In another medium bowl, beat the egg whites until stiff and fold into the rested batter.

5 Heat the oil in a deep fat fryer to 180°C / 350°F. The oil is hot enough when bubbles rise from the handle of a wooden spoon dipped into the fat.

6 Working in batches, dip the shrimp (prawns) in the batter, shake off the excess and deep-fry for about 3 minutes until golden brown. Drain on paper towels and keep warm.

7 Spoon the rice onto plates and scatter with the cashew nuts. Arrange the shrimp on top and serve at once.

SHRIMP AND MANGO CURRY

Ingredients

2 mangoes

3 tbsp grated coconut

3 tbsp coconut milk

A good pinch of chili powder

2 tbsp curry powder

2 tbsp sesame oil, plus some for seasoning

1 carrot, finely diced

2 onions, finely diced

3 garlic cloves, very finely diced

2 stalks celery, with leaves, diced finely, reserve a few leaves

1 lb 2 oz / 500 g large shrimp or prawns

Juice of ½ lemon

Salt & freshly milled pepper

Method

Prep and cook time: 30 min

1 Peel the mangoes and cut the flesh away from the stone in slices about ¼ inch (5 mm) thick.

2 Put half the mango flesh into a blender with the grated coconut, coconut milk, chili powder, curry powder and 3 tablespoons of water and blend to a fine purée.

3 Heat the sesame oil and briefly sauté the diced vegetables. Add the shrimp and sauté briefly. Stir in the puréed mango sauce and simmer gently for about 8 minutes. If the sauce becomes too thick, thin with a little coconut milk or warm water.

4 Season the seafood curry with lemon juice, sesame oil, salt and pepper. Serve garnished with the remaining mango slices and celery leaves.

VEGETARIAN
AND
VEGETABLE DISHES

STIR-FRIED VEGETABLES WITH TOFU

Ingredients

2 tsp vegetable oil, divided

1 lb / 450 g extra firm tofu, cut into cubes

4 shallots, quartered

2 garlic cloves, crushed

1 inch / 3-cm piece fresh ginger root, peeled and grated

1 cup / 200 g baby corn

8 oz / 200 g snow peas (mangetout)

2 cups / 200 g bean sprouts

8 oz / 200 g oyster and/or shiitake mushrooms, halved if large

1 cup / 225 ml vegetable broth (stock)

1 tbsp dark brown sugar

1 tbsp light soy sauce

2 tsp cornstarch (cornflour), mixed to a smooth paste in 2 tbsp water

Method

Prep and cook time: 20 min

1   In a nonstick skillet, heat 1 teaspoon of the oil over medium-high heat until hot. Add tofu and cook, gently for about 4 minutes, tossing until lightly golden. Transfer to a plate and set aside.

2   Meanwhile, heat the remaining teaspoon of oil in a large skillet or wok. Add the shallots, garlic, ginger, corn, snow peas, bean sprouts and mushrooms. Cook for 5 minutes, stirring frequently.

3   Add the tofu to the wok. Pour in the broth (stock), sugar, soy sauce and cornstarch (cornflour) mixture. Heat to boiling and cook for 2 minutes until the sauce thickens. Serve at once.

VEGETABLE NOODLES

Ingredients

For the curry paste:

1 red chili

1 clove garlic

¾ inch / 2 cm galangal, peeled

Good pinch grated peel of kaffir lime

1 tsp shrimp paste

For the vegetable noodles:

12–14 oz / 350–400 g mie noodles

8–10 oz / 250–300 g shiitake mushrooms

2 red bell peppers

1 scallion (spring onion)

1 tbsp vegetable oil

¾–1 cup / 200 ml coconut milk

3 sprigs Thai basil

1 tsp fish sauce

Salt & freshly milled pepper

Method

Prep and cook time: 25 min

1 Put all the curry paste ingredients into a mortar and grind to a paste.

2 Cook the noodles in plenty of boiling, salted water according to the package instructions until al dente.

3 Clean and slice the mushrooms. Wash, trim, halve and core the bell peppers and cut into strips. Trim the scallion (spring onion), cut into strips lengthways and cut the strips into 1-inch (3-cm) lengths.

4 Heat the vegetable oil and sauté the vegetables. Stir in 1–2 tablespoons curry paste and the coconut milk and simmer for 3–5 minutes.

5 Strip the Thai basil leaves from the stalks and add to the vegetables.

6 Season to taste with salt, pepper and fish sauce and add a little water if necessary.

7 Drain the noodles and put into bowls. Divide the vegetables between the bowls and serve hot.

NOODLES WITH PEANUT SAUCE AND TOFU

Ingredients

For the peanut sauce:

½ cup / 100 g unsalted peanuts, toasted and finely chopped

2 shallots, finely chopped

2 garlic cloves, finely chopped

3 tbsp sweet soy sauce

Juice of ½ lemon

1 tsp chili paste

1 tbsp sugar

2 tbsp groundnut oil

1¼ cups / 300 ml coconut milk

Salt

For the noodles:

1 lb / 450 g oriental wheat flour noodles

8 oz / 225 g red cabbage, chopped into fine strips

1 red bell pepper, deseeded and chopped into strips.

4 scallions (spring onions), chopped into rings

4 carrots, chopped into fine strips

8 oz / 225 g tofu, chopped into cubes

Method
Prep and cook time: 40 min

1 To make the sauce, place the peanuts, shallots, garlic, soy sauce, lemon juice, chili paste and sugar in a tall mixing beaker and purée to a creamy paste using a hand-held blender.

2 Heat the groundnut oil in a pan and briefly fry the peanut paste. Pour in the coconut milk, stir until smooth then simmer for about 3 minutes until slightly thickened. Season with salt.

3 Cook the noodles according to the package instructions. Drain and divide between four plates.

4 Spoon the sauce over the noodles, scatter with the red cabbage and pepper strips, scallions (spring onions), carrot strips and tofu, and serve.

RICE WITH ONIONS, MUSHROOMS AND EGG

Ingredients

1 1/3 cups / 250 g long-grain rice

3 tbsp vegetable oil

8 scallions (spring onions), sliced diagonally into rings (reserve a few for garnish)

2 cups / 250 g halved mushrooms

6 eggs

Freshly ground pepper, to taste

2 tbsp light soy sauce, plus more to taste

Sliced scallion (spring onion), to garnish

Method

Prep and cook time: 40 min

1 Cook the rice according to the instructions on the package and let cool completely.

2 Heat the oil in a wok or skillet. Add the scallion (spring onion) rings and stir-fry for 2 minutes. Add the mushrooms and stir-fry until all liquid has evaporated.

3 Add the rice and cook, stirring, about 3 minutes, then push the rice mixture to the edges of the wok.

4 In a small bowl, whisk the eggs and season with pepper and 2 tbsp soy sauce. Pour into the center of the wok and cook quickly, stirring constantly. Lightly mix the eggs through the rice and season with soy sauce, to taste. Scatter with the reserved scallion rings and serve at once.

LENTIL AND POTATO CURRY

Ingredients

2 tsp ghee or clarified butter

1 onion, finely chopped

2 clove garlic, finely chopped

Walnut-size piece fresh ginger, peeled and grated

1 tsp curcuma (turmeric)

½ tsp cayenne pepper

½ tsp ground coriander

½ tsp cumin

1 lb / 450 g waxy potatoes, roughly chopped

8 oz / 225 g pumpkin flesh, roughly chopped

1¼ cups / 250 g lentils, rinsed and drained

1¼ cups / 250 g canned tomatoes, chopped

Salt

2 tbsp cilantro (fresh coriander), to garnish

Method
Prep and cook time: 50 min

1 Sweat the onion and garlic with the ginger, curcuma (turmeric), cayenne pepper, coriander and cumin in hot ghee for 4–5 minutes, stirring occasionally.

2 Add the potatoes, pumpkin, lentils, tomatoes and just enough water to cover all the ingredients. Cover and simmer gently for 30–40 minutes, stirring occasionally and ensuring that the pan does not boil dry.

3 Season with salt and serve garnished with cilantro (fresh coriander) leaves.

CURRY MEE WITH TOFU

Ingredients

14 oz / 400 g tofu, smoked or plain
according to taste

9 oz / 250 g Chinese egg noodles

5 tbsp vegetable oil

Scant 1 cup / 200 ml unsweetened
coconut milk, more if necessary

2 red chilis, deseeded and finely
chopped

2 cloves garlic, finely chopped

½ tsp pepper

2 tbsp curry powder

1 handful bean sprouts

2 tbsp light soy sauce

1 tbsp vinegar

1 tbsp sugar

2 tbsp fish sauce

Method

Prep and cook time: 35 min

1 Dice the tofu and drain on paper towel.

2 Put the noodles into a bowl and soak in lukewarm water.

3 Heat the oil and brown the tofu on all sides for 2–3 minutes. Add the coconut milk.

4 Add the chilies and the garlic to the pan with the spices and bring to a boil.

5 Drain the noodles, break into smaller pieces if necessary and add to the pan. Cook gently in the hot sauce for 3–4 minutes, until done. Mix in the bean sprouts and warm in the sauce. Add soy sauce, vinegar, sugar and fish sauce to taste. Divide between 4 small bowls and serve hot.

PALAK PANEER

Ingredients

14 oz / 400 g paneer cheese

4 tbsp ghee or clarified butter

2 onions, finely chopped

2 cloves garlic, finely chopped

1 tsp ginger, freshly grated

½ tsp ground coriander

½ tsp ground turmeric

½ tsp ground cumin

½ tsp chili powder

2¼ lb / 1 kg spinach, roughly chopped

⅔ cup / 150 ml cream

Salt

Method

Prep and cook time: 25 min

1 Dice the paneer cheese. Heat half of the ghee (or clarified butter) in a skillet and fry the paneer until golden brown. Set aside.

2 Sauté the onion, garlic and ginger in the rest of the ghee until golden brown. Stir in the spices, then add the spinach, cover and cook for about 10 minutes. Then add the cream (apart from 4 tablespoons) and the paneer and simmer for a further 5 minutes or so. Season to taste with salt and serve drizzled with the rest of the cream.

KORMA WITH SAFFRON RICE

Ingredients

1¼ cups / 250 g basmati and wild rice mixture

¼ tsp ground saffron

1 onion, finely chopped

2 tbsp ghee or clarified butter

1 tsp curcuma (turmeric)

½ tsp cumin

½ tsp ground ginger

²/₃ cup / 150 ml vegetable broth (stock)

2 cups / 600 g cauliflower florets

²/₃ cup / 100 g peeled almonds, roughly chopped

2 carrots, peeled and roughly chopped

2 cups / 200 g canned chick peas, rinsed and drained

²/₃ cup / 150 ml yogurt

8 oz / 225 g fresh spinach, rinsed and spun dry

Salt and freshly ground pepper

Method

Prep and cook time: 40 min.

1 Cook the rice with the saffron in salted water according to the package instructions.

2 Sweat the onion in hot ghee. Add the curcuma (turmeric), cumin and ginger and continue frying for a few minutes then pour in the vegetable broth (stock).

3 Add the cauliflower, almonds, carrots and chick peas, season with salt, cover and simmer for about 15 minutes, stirring occasionally, until the vegetables are cooked through.

4 Stir in the yogurt and spinach, remove from the heat and season with salt and pepper.

5 Divide the rice between 4 plates and top with the curry.

RICE NOODLES
WITH CABBAGE AND
RED COCONUT SAUCE

Ingredients

1 tbsp sesame oil

1 shallot, finely chopped

2 garlic cloves, finely chopped

½ tsp chili powder

½ tsp curcuma (turmeric)

½ tsp ground paprika

½ tsp ground five-spice powder

Scant 1 cup / 200 ml coconut milk

2 tbsp lime juice

½ cup / 125 ml vegetable broth (stock)

1 lb / 450 g savoy cabbage, chopped into strips or torn into bite-size pieces

½ cup / 50 g soybean shoots

8 oz / 225 g rice noodles

Salt

Method

Prep and cook time: 30 min

1 Fry the shallots and garlic in sesame oil.

2 Add the chili powder, curcuma (turmeric), paprika and five-spice powder and fry briefly then add the coconut milk, lime juice and vegetable broth (stock). Simmer gently for about 5 minutes and season with salt.

3 Add the savoy cabbage and simmer gently for a further 5–7 minutes. Last of all, add the soybean shoots and warm through for 1–2 minutes.

4 Cook the rice noodles in plenty of water according to the package instructions and drain.

5 Divide the noodles between four bowls and top with the savoy cabbage in coconut sauce.

PUNJABI STYLE CHICK PEAS

Ingredients

10 oz / 300 g dried chick peas, soaked overnight and drained

4 tbsp olive oil

4 shallots, sliced into rings

1 garlic clove, sliced

½ tsp cumin

½ tsp ground coriander

1 tsp garam masala

½ tsp curcuma (turmeric)

8 oz / 225 g floury potatoes, peeled and chopped

2 tomatoes, roughly chopped

2 chili peppers

2 tbsp cilantro (fresh coriander), chopped

Cayenne pepper

Salt

Method

Prep and cook time: 2 h 20 min
plus overnight soaking

1 Cover the chick peas with 5 cups (1¼ liters) of water and simmer over a low heat for 1½ hours until soft.

2 Fry the shallots in hot oil until golden brown, and reserve 1 tbsp to garnish.

3 Add the garlic, cumin, ground coriander, garam masala and curcuma (turmeric) to the shallots in the pan and fry briefly.

4 Add the potatoes, drained chick peas and about 100 ml (scant ½ cup) of water.

5 Add the tomatoes and chili peppers, cover and simmer gently for about 30 minutes, stirring occasionally. Add a little more water if necessary.

6 Season to taste with salt and cayenne pepper and stir in the chopped cilantro (fresh coriander).

7 Spoon into bowls and serve garnished with the reserved onions.

ORIENTAL NOODLE BAKE

Ingredients

8 oz / 225 g mie noodles

1 clove garlic, chopped

1²/₃ cups / 400 ml coconut milk

2 tbsp soy sauce

Cayenne pepper

3 eggs

¼ oz / 5 g dried mu err mushrooms, soaked in water according to package instructions

3 tbsp butter

8 oz / 225 g snow peas (mangetout), halved

2 carrots, pared into very thin slices with a peeler

4 scallions (spring onions), chopped into rings

1 red bell pepper, deseeded and finely sliced

2 tbsp chopped cilantro (fresh coriander)

2–3 tbsp bread crumbs

Cilantro (fresh coriander) leaves, to garnish

Method
Prep and cook time: 1 hour

1 Preheat the oven to 200C (400F / Gas Mark 6).

2 Cook the noodles according to the package instructions, refresh and drain.

3 Mix together the garlic and coconut milk, season to taste with some of the soy sauce and some cayenne pepper and stir in the eggs.

4 Drain the mushrooms, pat dry and chop into fine slices.

5 Heat 1 tbsp of butter in a skillet and fry the snow peas (mangetout) with 2–3 tbsp of water for 2–3 minutes. Add the carrots and fry for a further 2 minutes.

6 Stir in the scallions (spring onions), bell peppers, mushrooms and chopped cilantro (fresh coriander) and season with soy sauce.

7 Place the noodles into a greased ovenproof dish and spread the vegetable mixture on top.

8 Pour over the coconut sauce, sprinkle with bread crumbs, dot with the remaining butter and bake for about 20 minutes.

9 Garnish with cilantro (fresh coriander) leaves and serve.

LENTIL CURRY WITH PANEER

Ingredients

2 onions

2 cloves garlic

2 tbsp ghee or clarified butter

1 tsp curcuma (turmeric)

Pinch of ground cloves

Pinch of ground cumin

Pinch of ground allspice

2 curry leaves

1 cup / 250 ml unsweetened coconut milk

1¾ cups / about 400 ml vegetable broth (stock)

1 cup / 200 g black lentils

1 cup / 200 g red lentils

Salt & freshly milled pepper

7 oz / 200 g paneer cheese

Method

Prep and cook time: 40 min

1 Peel and finely chop the onions and garlic. Heat the ghee (or clarified butter) and sauté the onions and garlic, add the spices and sauté briefly before pouring in the coconut milk. Stir in a little broth (stock) and the black lentils, cover and simmer gently for about 10 minutes.

2 Add the red lentils and a little more broth. Simmer for a further 15 minutes or so, stirring occasionally and add the rest of the broth as necessary.

3 Remove the curry leaves and season to taste with salt and pepper.

4 Dice the paneer and add to the curry. Serve with flatbread.

SAAG ALOO

Ingredients

1 lb 2 oz / 500 g potatoes, peeled and cut into bite-size pieces

1 tbsp oil

1 tsp black mustard seeds

1 onion, finely diced

2 cloves garlic, finely chopped

1 tsp ginger, freshly grated

1 tsp chili powder

2 limes

1 lb 2 oz / 500 g fresh spinach

Method

Prep and cook time: 30 min

1 Parboil the potatoes in salted water for 10 minutes then drain.

2 Heat 1 tsp of the oil in a nonstick skillet, add the mustard seeds and toast briefly. Add the diced onion, garlic and ginger and fry for 1–2 minutes, stirring constantly. Add the chili powder, potatoes, the juice of one lime and a scant ¼ cup / 50 ml water.

3 Put a lid on the pan and cook the potatoes over a low heat for about 15 minutes, take care that the pan does not boil dry. Wash and drain the spinach, add to the pan and mix with the potatoes. Cook for about 3 minutes, until the spinach has wilted.

4 Check the seasoning and serve onto plates. Cut the remaining lime into wedges and add to the dish as a garnish.

EGGPLANT AND SNOW PEA CURRY

Ingredients

1 cup / 150 g snow peas (mangetout), trimmed

1 green chili

1½ inch / 4 cm lemongrass

1 clove garlic

1 kaffir lime leaf

2 shallots, finely chopped

2 tbsp oil

1 cup / 250 ml vegetable broth (stock)

1 cup / 250 ml unsweetened coconut milk

6 Thai eggplants (aubergines), roughly chopped

1 lb 2 oz / 500 g sweet potatoes, peeled and diced

½ an untreated lime, juice and zest

Light soy sauce

Honey

Salt

Method
Prep and cook time: 30 min

1 Blanch the snow peas (mangetout) in boiling salted water until al dente. Place immediately into cold water then drain.

2 Crush the lemongrass, chili, peeled garlic and kaffir lime leaf to a smooth paste using a pestle and mortar.

3 Sauté the shallots in hot oil with the curry paste. Pour in the vegetable broth (stock) and the coconut milk and simmer for about 5 minutes. Add the eggplant and the sweet potatoes and simmer for 10 minutes, stirring occasionally. Add the lime juice, lime zest and snow peas and season to taste with soy sauce, honey, and salt before serving.

RIBBON NOODLES WITH COCONUT CURRY SAUCE

Ingredients

Curry paste:

2 dried chilis

1 shallot, peeled

¾ inch / 2 cm coriander root

¾ inch / 2 cm lemongrass

Good pinch of cumin seeds

½ tsp curcuma (turmeric)

1 lb 2 oz / 500 g ribbon noodles

1 tbsp oil

1 onion, finely chopped

1–2 cloves garlic, finely chopped

Juice and finely grated zest of 1 lime

1¾ cup / 400 ml unsweetened coconut milk

1–2 tbsp fish sauce

Salt & white pepper

Sugar

Parsley leaves, to garnish

Method

Prep and cook time: 40 min

1 Put all the ingredients for the curry paste into a mortar and crush to a paste.

2 Cook the ribbon noodles according to the package instructions until al dente.

3 Meanwhile heat the oil and sauté the chopped onion and garlic until translucent. Add the lime zest and stir in the coconut milk. Stir in the lime juice, curry paste and fish sauce and season to taste with salt, pepper and sugar. Simmer the sauce gently for about 5 minutes, until it has a creamy consistency. Remove from the heat and blend with a hand blender.

4 Drain the cooked noodles, mix at once with the coconut curry sauce and serve garnished with parsley leaves.

DHAL WITH COCONUT AND RAISINS

Ingredients

1–2 tbsp raisins

9 oz / 250 g split chick peas (channa dal)

1–2 tsp curcuma (turmeric)

A good pinch of chili powder

2 green chilis

2 tbsp jaggery (or brown sugar)

½ tsp ground coriander

½ tsp ground cumin

1–2 tsp garam masala

A good pinch of salt

2–3 tbsp ghee or clarified butter

1 cup / 100 g coconut flakes

Method

Prep and cook time: 1 hour

1 Wash the raisins and put into a cup of hot water to soak. Wash the chickpeas in cold water and put into a pan with the curcuma (turmeric), chili powder and 4 cups (1 liter) of water. Bring to a boil, cover and cook over a low heat for about 30 minutes.

2 Trim and halve the chilis, remove the inner ribs and the seeds if you wish, and cut into rings. Stir into the chick peas with the jaggery, coriander, cumin and 1 tsp garam masala. Add the salt and cook for a further 10–15 minutes, until the chickpeas are very soft.

3 Heat the ghee (or clarified butter) in a skillet and lightly toast the rest of the garam masala and the coconut flakes. Mix into the dhal with the drained raisins. Spoon into bowls and serve with rice.

QUICK VEGETABLE CURRY

Ingredients

2 cups / 300 g green beans, trimmed

4 carrots, peeled and cut into batons

3 cups / 600 g broccoli, cut into florets

Oil

1–2 tbsp yellow curry paste, from an Asian grocery store

2 garlic cloves, finely chopped

1 can coconut milk

1 red bell pepper, de-seeded and cut into strips

Chili, according to taste

Salt

Cilantro (coriander) sprigs, to garnish

Method

Prep and cook time: 35 min

1 Blanch the beans for 8 minutes in boiling, salted water, the carrots for 5 minutes and the broccoli florets for 4 minutes. Drain the vegetables well.

2 Heat the curry paste with 1 tablespoon of oil in a skillet. Sauté the garlic, then pour in the coconut milk. Bring to a boil, then reduce the heat and add the bell pepper. Simmer for about 3 minutes.

3 Add the broccoli, green beans and carrots and simmer for a further 2–3 minutes. Season to taste with chili and salt.

4 Garnish the vegetable curry with fresh cilantro (coriander) sprigs and serve with rice.

POTATO CURRY
WITH ZUCCHINI AND CASHEW NUTS

Ingredients

3 cups / 500 g small zucchini (courgettes)

1½ cups / 300 g tomatoes

2 lb 4 oz / 1 kg boiling potatoes

1 red onion

1 clove garlic

1 oz / 25 g ginger

2 tbsp ghee or clarified butter

1 tbsp curry powder, according to taste

1 tsp ground cumin

Salt & freshly milled pepper

2 cups / 500 ml vegetable broth (stock)

1 tbsp potato starch

½ cup / 60 g cashew nuts, roasted

Method

Prep and cook time: 45 min

1 Trim the zucchini (courgettes) and cut into cubes. Cut the tomatoes into quarters and de-seed. Peel the potatoes and dice. Blanch the potatoes in boiling salted water for 8 minutes, then drain. Peel the onion and the garlic and chop. Peel the ginger and finely chop.

2 Fry the potatoes in hot ghee or clarified butter. Add the zucchini and sauté, then stir in the garlic, onion and ginger and fry. Season with curry powder, cumin, salt and pepper. Now add the tomatoes and pour in the vegetable broth (stock). Simmer for 15–20 minutes.

3 Mix the potato starch to a paste with a drop of cold water, then stir the mixture into the hot curry. Bring to a boil, then simmer and season to taste.

4 Sprinkle a few roasted cashew nuts over the top and serve on warmed plates.

CHEESE AND BROCCOLI TIKKIS

Ingredients

1 tbsp oil plus oil for frying

¾ cup / 125 g finely chopped onions

2 cloves garlic, finely chopped

1–2 green chilis, finely chopped

1½ cups / 300 g broccoli florets, finely chopped

2–3 tbsp cornstarch (cornflour)

¾ cup / 70 g finely grated cheese

9 oz / 250 g baking potatoes, cooked and mashed

2 cups / 100 g breadcrumbs

Salt

For the yogurt dip:

Generous 1 cup / 300 g plain yogurt

1 tsp tandoori masala spices mix

Method

Prep and cook time: 1 hour

1 Heat one tablespoon oil in a skillet and sauté the onions, garlic and chili. Add the broccoli and cook for 4–5 minutes, then season with salt. Stir in the cornstarch (cornflour) and the cheese, mix well, then let cool.

2 Combine with the mashed potatoes. Divide into 8 equal portions and form into round patties.

3 Coat the patties with breadcrumbs. Heat the frying oil in a large skillet and fry the tikkis on both sides until golden brown.

4 To make the yogurt dip, simply mix the yogurt with a teaspoonful of tandoori masala spices mix and serve with the tikkis.

CHINESE SPICED EGGPLANT

Ingredients

4 small eggplants (aubergines)

1 1/3 cups / 300 ml vegetable oil

1 tbsp sugar

2 tbsp rice vinegar

2 tsp soy sauce

2 tbsp rice wine

2 tsp cornstarch (cornflour), mixed to a smooth paste in 1 tbsp water

1 tbsp spicy (hot) bean paste

1 inch / 3-cm piece fresh ginger root, minced

2 cloves garlic, minced

1/4 leek, finely chopped

Method

Prep and cook time: 30 min

1 Trim the eggplants (aubergines) and cut each lengthwise into 6 wedges.

2 Heat the oil in a wok or skillet. Add the eggplant in batches and deep-fry for about 3 minutes, until golden brown. Drain on paper towels and keep warm on a plate.

3 In a small bowl, mix the sugar with the vinegar, soy sauce, rice wine and cornstarch (cornflour) paste to make a sauce.

4 Pour off and discard the oil in the wok, leaving behind a thin film. Add the bean paste, ginger and garlic and stir-fry for 30 seconds. Stir in the sauce and 1 tbsp water. Bring to a boil and stir in the leeks.

5 Pour the hot sauce over the eggplant wedges and serve.

SICHUAN STYLE BEANS
WITH GINGER AND GARLIC

Ingredients

2 tbsp vegetable oil

1 lb / 450 g Chinese long beans (yard-long beans) or green beans, trimmed and cut into 2 inch / 5-cm lengths

2 garlic cloves, chopped

3 cm / 1-inch piece fresh ginger root, peeled and grated

½ tsp chili paste

1 tbsp light soy sauce

Pinch of sugar

Salt and freshly ground black pepper, to taste

Cilantro (fresh coriander) leaves, to garnish

Method

Prep and cook time: 20 min

1 Heat the oil in a large wok or skillet, add the beans and stir-fry for 3 minutes or until they start to soften.

2 Add the garlic, ginger and chili paste and stir-fry for 30 seconds, then stir in the soy sauce, sugar, salt and pepper. Garnish with cilantro (coriander) leaves and serve at once.

SWEET POTATO STICKS WITH SESAME SAUCE

Ingredients

3 tbsp sesame seeds

6 tbsp honey

3 tsp lemon juice

5½ cups / 800 g sweet potatoes, chopped into ¼-inch / 5 mm strips

Vegetable oil for deep frying

Method

Prep and cook time: 30 min

1 Toast the sesame seeds, stirring constantly in a dry skillet over medium-high heat until golden brown. Transfer to a plate to cool.

2 In a small saucepan, heat the honey and lemon juice and stir until smooth. Add the toasted sesame seeds and let cool slightly.

3 Heat the oil in a deep fat fryer to 350°F / 180°C.

4 Pat dry the sweet potato sticks with paper towels, then deep-fry in batches in the hot oil for about 10 minutes or until golden. Drain on paper towels.

5 Arrange the sweet potato sticks on a plate and drizzle with a little honey and sesame sauce. Serve the rest of the sauce as a dip.

SWEET AND SOUR GREEN BEANS

Ingredients

2 lb 4 oz / 1 kg green beans, trimmed and cut into 2-inch / 5-cm lengths

Vegetable oil, for deep-frying

2 garlic cloves, minced

2 chili peppers, seeded and chopped

2 scallions (spring onions), finely chopped

1 inch / 3-cm piece fresh ginger root, peeled and grated

1 cup / 100 g canned kidney beans, rinsed and drained

2 tbsp rice wine

2 tbsp fish sauce

Soy sauce, to taste

Method

Prep and cook time: 45 min

1 Heat the oil in a deep fat fryer to 350°F / 180°C. Working in batches, deep-fry the beans until they begin to wrinkle. Drain the beans on paper towels and keep warm.

2 Heat 2 tbsp of the oil in another wok or skillet; add the garlic, chili peppers, scallions (spring onions) and ginger. Stir-fry for 1 minute, then add the kidney beans, 2–3 tbsp water, the rice wine and fish sauce and simmer for 1–2 minutes.

3 Add the green beans and season with soy sauce; heat through and serve at once.

CHINESE BROCCOLI
WITH ORANGE

Ingredients

1 head broccoli, stems peeled and cut into small florets

Finely grated zest and juice of 1 orange

2 tsp cornstarch (cornflour)

1 tbsp light soy sauce

½ tsp sugar

2 tbsp olive oil

1 inch / 3-cm piece fresh ginger root, peeled and cut into thin slivers

2 garlic cloves, chopped

1 cup / 100 g bean sprouts

Method

Prep and cook time: 20 min

1 Bring a large pot of water to a boil. Add the broccoli and blanch for 30 seconds; drain in a colander under cold running water to stop the cooking. Drain and set aside.

2 To prepare the sauce, in a small bowl, mix the orange juice and zest with 4 tbsp water, the cornstarch (cornflour), soy sauce and sugar and set aside.

3 Heat the oil in a wok or large skillet; add the ginger and garlic and stir-fry for 10 seconds. Add the broccoli and stir-fry for 2 minutes more. Add the bean sprouts and cook for 1 more minute.

4 Stir the orange sauce mixture into the wok and cook, stirring constantly, until the sauce has thickened and coated the broccoli. Spoon into a serving dish and serve at once.

SPICY EGGPLANT

Ingredients

2 lb 4 oz / 1 kg Thai eggplants (aubergines)

4–6 fresh red chilies

¼ cup / 60 ml oil

²/₃ cup / 150 ml vegetable broth (stock)

1–1¼ cup / 160–200 g bamboo shoots, cut into thin strips

Salt and freshly milled pepper

Method

Prep and cook time: 20 min

1 Halve some of the Thai eggplants (aubergines) and halve the chilis lengthways. Lightly prick the whole eggplants several times so that they do not burst during cooking.

2 Heat the oil in a wok and add the chilies. Then add the eggplants and fry on all sides for 3–4 minutes, until lightly browned.

3 Add the broth (stock) and cook for a further 3–4 minutes, until done, adding the bamboo shoots after 2 minutes. If the eggplants are still too firm, cook for up to 5 minutes more.

4 Season to taste with salt and pepper and serve in bowls.

Published by Transatlantic Press

First published in 2010

Transatlantic Press
38 Copthorne Road, Croxley Green, Hertfordshire WD3 4AQ

© Transatlantic Press

Images and Recipes by StockFood © The Food Image Agency

ISBN 978-1-907176-60-9

Printed in China